Walking
Ireland's
Mountains

Walking
Ireland's
Mountains

A GUIDE TO THE RANGES
AND THE BEST
WALKING ROUTES

DAVID HERMAN

Appletree Press

Published by

The Appletree Press Ltd

19-21 Alfred Street

Belfast BT2 8DL

1994

British Library Cataloguing-in-Publication Data

A catalogue record for this book is

available from the British Library.

ISBN 0 86281 459 6 (pbk)

ISBN 0 86281 471 5 (hbk)

9 8 7 6 5 4 3 2 1

CONTENTS

. . . .

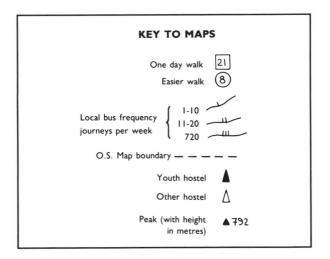

KEY TO MAPS

One day walk   21

Easier walk   ⑧

Local bus frequency   {   1-10
journeys per week   11-20
                    720

O.S. Map boundary — — — — —

Youth hostel   ▲

Other hostel   △

Peak (with height   ▲ 792
in metres)

ACKNOWLEDGEMENTS

I would like to thank Jean Boydell for information about the Knockmealdowns, Tom Dalton for the Galtees, Sean O Suilleabhain and Dr Catherine McMullin for the mountains of Kerry, Maurice Simms for the Sperrins and the Antrim Plateau, Liam Reinhardt for the mountains of Mayo. In particular, I am pleased to thank Malcolm Hunt for his invaluable comments and encouragement at a crucial stage in this project.

I greatly appreciate the help and unfailing courtesy of Malachy McVeigh and Harry McDermott of the Ordnance Survey in Dublin in providing information about the OS maps.

Among others who offered help and information, I would like to thank especially Gerry Butler, Paul Hudson, Paul Kavanagh, Karl Marshall, Cathal Lalor, Eddie McGrane and Kevin O'Loughlin.

The extract from *The Mountains of Ireland* by Daphne Pochin Mould is given with permission of the publishers Gill & Macmillan; that from *Hamish's Groats End Walk* by Hamish Brown with the permission of the publishers Victor Gollancz; that from *Around Ireland in Slow Gear* by Eric Newby with permission of the publishers HarperCollins; and that from *Sunrise with Seamonsters* by Paul Theroux with permission by Cape. I offer my sincere thanks to all concerned.

Lastly, not for the first time, thanks are due to my wife Mairin Geraty for her support in many ways, not least of which her cheerful acceptance of the occasional trudge over dreary bogland in the drizzling rain in the arduous course of "research".

The representation in this book of a road, track or footpath is not evidence of the existence of a right of way.

While every care has been taken to describe the routes and the terrain accurately, the publisher and author can take no responsibility for any loss, injury or inconvenience sustained as a result of using this guide.

INTRODUCTION

As well as giving brief descriptions of some of the best hill walking routes, this short guide is primarily intended to give an *overview* of the Irish mountains, the wood rather than the trees, or more appropriately in this instance the range rather than the peaks. It is therefore aimed at walkers, whether visitors or natives, who want a general idea of what each mountain area has to offer.

In this book the entire island is divided into eight regions (the term "region" is used only in this context, and their boundaries do not always fully accord with established usage), each of which, assuming the availability of a car, can be explored from just a few centres.

I have taken a brutally frank approach to descriptions of the mountain ranges, on the grounds that if *everywhere* is described as superlatively beautiful and exhilaratingly challenging, the bemused reader will be no wiser at the end than at the start of the book. Some might reasonably counter this by claiming that *all* mountain areas in Ireland are superlatively beautiful and exhilaratingly challenging – a view with which I have some sympathy.

I have visited all the mountain ranges mentioned in these pages and have explored parts, at least, of all of them – not so difficult a feat since I have wandered Ireland's mountains for nearly thirty years. There is no objectivity in the evaluation of the beauty and attractiveness of the mountains – or anything else – so the evaluations in this book are mine and mine alone, and yours could well be quite different. I can only hope that your impressions agree with those given. Regardless of any criticism meted out in these pages, there are lovely days' walking to be had in even the most modest of the Irish mountain ranges. Given favourable weather, the dullest of ranges can be memorable – just as in bad weather, the most spectacular will be dispiriting.

The other topics discussed in this book are listed in the contents page and need not be tediously repeated here. However, attention might perhaps be drawn to the sections on Further Reading at the end of the regional chapters, as well as the bibliograpy. These are particularly detailed as befits a book whose aim is to encourage further exploration, both literary and later, it is hoped, on the ground.

May I wish you happy and satisfying days in Ireland's mountains!

IN PRAISE OF IRELAND'S MOUNTAINS

Though I have absolutely no evidence to back up this large claim, I would be surprised if there are many who have come hill walking to Ireland and, if they have enjoyed even moderately good weather (admittedly a big if), have returned home disappointed. Every person who is sufficiently analytical to consider the subject will have a different set of reasons for this favourable impression, but perhaps I could suggest just four which may encourage you to try hill walking in Ireland, if you have not already done so.

In four words they are: beauty, variability, accessibility and remoteness. The first two are so evident that they scarcely need any elaboration, though they should be considered in conjunction with each other. Beauty without variation, no matter how stunning, can ultimately pall and become uninteresting. In many mountain places, each few steps bring another hill into view and open up a vista of a corrie lake or a tumbling stream. Variety is certainly the spice of beauty.

Accessibility and remoteness seem at first glance to be strange bed-fellows. Not really so. Most Irish mountains are close to a motorable road and few are far from good centres. There is no need for long treks and highly organised expeditions. Yet when you get into the mountains, you are very soon in remote areas: no houses or mountain huts, few tracks or other walkers. Remoteness *with* accessibility – an attractive combination!

This brings us to the eight regions into which I have grouped the Irish mountain ranges. On page 12 is a summary

REGION	TERRAIN	EXTENT	AMBIENCE	FACILITIES	MAPS
South-East	🌲	🌲🌲	🌲	🌲🌲🌲🌲	🌲
Wicklow	🌲🌲	🌲🌲🌲🌲	🌲	🌲🌲🌲	🌲🌲🌲
Northern Ireland					
Mournes	🌲🌲🌲	🌲🌲	🌲	🌲🌲🌲🌲	🌲🌲🌲🌲
Rest	🌲	🌲	🌲	🌲🌲🌲🌲	🌲🌲🌲🌲
Donegal	🌲🌲🌲	🌲🌲🌲	🌲🌲🌲🌲	🌲🌲	🌲🌲🌲🌲
North Connaught	🌲🌲	🌲	🌲🌲	🌲🌲🌲	🌲🌲🌲
Mayo					
South	🌲🌲🌲	🌲🌲	🌲🌲🌲🌲	🌲	🌲🌲🌲🌲
Rest	🌲🌲	🌲🌲🌲	🌲🌲🌲🌲	🌲	🌲🌲
Connemara					
Bens	🌲🌲🌲🌲	🌲🌲🌲	🌲🌲🌲🌲	🌲🌲	🌲🌲🌲🌲
Burren	🌲🌲	🌲	🌲	🌲🌲🌲	🌲🌲
Rest	🌲🌲	🌲🌲	🌲🌲🌲	🌲🌲	🌲🌲🌲🌲
Kerry					
Dingle	🌲🌲🌲	🌲🌲	🌲🌲🌲	🌲🌲	🌲🌲🌲🌲
Iveragh	🌲🌲🌲🌲	🌲🌲🌲🌲	🌲🌲🌲🌲	🌲🌲	🌲🌲🌲
Beara	🌲🌲	🌲🌲	🌲🌲🌲	🌲	🌲🌲

Symbols indicating quality are graded from 🌲 (worst) to 🌲🌲🌲🌲 (best).

The following terms are used.

TERRAIN: beauty, dramatic quality and underfoot conditions.

EXTENT: possibilities of long walks or shorter but arduous ones.

AMBIENCE: remoteness and wildness of area around mountains.

FACILITIES: accommodation, road system, public transport.

MAPS: availability in early 1994.

of the natural and infrastructural characteristics of each region. The purpose of this is to allow you to roughly compare the regions before you look more closely at them. Please take into account that all subtleties have been erased, and more importantly, that this is only one person's fallible judgement.

One general point is evident from the summary: the distinction between the regions bordering the Atlantic seaboard, specifically Donegal, Mayo, Connemara and Kerry, and the rest of the country. The mountain ranges of these regions are surrounded not by agricultural land as elsewhere, but by wild moorland and sea, with its many convoluted inlets. These are mountains that are more remote and found in areas of the country that are less developed; but, once there, you will probably agree that the longer journey was worth the extra effort.

Having said so much that is positive, it is only fair to mention an endemic problem, one that I bring up with the utmost regret. If cleanliness is indeed next to godliness, then Irish are atheists. I can only ask your forebearance when faced by careless littering and even dumping. It is scant compensation to know that most native hill walkers feel just as strongly as I do about this problem and are doing their best to remedy it.

RIGHTS OF WAY AND GOOD CONDUCT

. . . .

In practice, but not legally, you can walk almost anywhere on Irish hills – as long as you behave properly. You have to be circumspect in the immediate vicinity of farm buildings; in Wicklow and the Mournes, which are within range of big city louts, some landowners are understandably on short fuses. Nearly everywhere else you have, in practice, the freedom of the hills on and off paths.

There is, however, a particular legal difficulty at the moment (early 1994). The position on public-liability insurance covering walkers on private land in the jurisdiction of the Republic of Ireland is most unsatisfactory, so much so that urgent steps are being taken to amend it. It is hoped that this will be a short-term problem; in the meantime, please be sympathetic about those few occasions where landowners have refused access to walkers. Do remember that regardless of the legal position, you are almost always on land that represents somebody's livelihood and you must behave accordingly. You have few legal rights; permission to walk across private land is at the discretion of landowners. They have a perfect right to ask trespassers, which is what walkers legally are, to leave their land. This very rarely happens and if it does it is probably for a good reason.

You can greatly ease access difficulties by your behaviour. Most aspects of good conduct (closing gates, no littering) should not need mentioning. I must emphasise, however, that you should not stand on fence strands, which may become irrevocably damaged, and you should not allow dogs loose in sheep-rearing areas (almost everywhere in the uplands). These two points are particularly important in Ireland.

What happens if you come across a stern notice ordering you to keep off what you assumed was a route open to walkers? It is very difficult to know, though you shouldn't assume that you should automatically turn back. If you are near a big city, it is certainly prudent to retreat; otherwise it depends. I have stood perplexed at a "No Entry" sign only to be informed by a most friendly local that the sign referred only to cars! Perhaps the best practical advice is to interpret whether the sign really refers to you; if you decide that it might not, ask a local person, while scrupulously obeying the guidelines outlined above. In fact, exchanging a few words of greeting with locals is always diplomatic – and you never know what you might learn!

PATHS AND TRACKS

Visiting hill walkers will be immediately aware of the lack of *purposeful* paths and tracks in most Irish mountain areas, except in Northern Ireland. Paths there are, but they are not very common, usually the result of random boots or sheep hooves rather than conscious design, seldom signposted and rarely indicated on the maps. This means a much greater reliance on map and compass than would otherwise be the case. While this may be at first a little off-putting, it does offer a chance to experience a more challenging form of hill walking, one which in the long haul should prove more interesting than merely following a predetermined route.

Ireland has a number of long-distance paths, only some of which are waymarked. While it is the intention to waymark them all eventually, several are indicated only on maps while others are not even so marked. The long-distance walking authorities in the two jurisdictions regularly issue updated leaflets on all the paths. The long-distance paths cover all types of country; paths that traverse mountain areas are mentioned at the appropriate point in the text.

THE ROUTES

. . . .

Brief route descriptions of a total of eighty one-day routes are grouped under each of the eight regions, and are shown in square boxes in the sketch maps. These route descriptions together with the map(s) specified, should be enough to enable a person with average navigational skills to complete the route in reasonable weather. Glancing through them, you may think that the route descriptions are very terse. However, they do give the most important points about route descriptions under Irish conditions. Included are: descriptions of the starting points and, in some cases, how to get to them; outlines of the routes into open country; a highlighting of all dangers and hazards in the terrain which are not obvious from the reference map(s) specified at the start of the routes; indications of useful paths in the mountains; mention of summit features, except cairns (which are very common) unless the cairns are important or special in some way. Besides these features (and of course assuming the walker has a map), only brief outlines of the routes are needed.

The routes given are nearly all one-day walks and are looped (with only a few exceptions) so that they require only one car. They are designed to give a good sample of the best and most characteristic mountains in each region, with "best" taking precedence over "characteristic". Because Ireland is not on the whole blessed with a perfect climate for walking, and because even the most enthusiastic walker might occasionally want an easy day, there is also a section under each region giving brief details of shorter walks. They are indicated in circular boxes on the sketch maps. In a few cases, they are given in the form of areas. These easier walks are particularly suitable for days of poor visibility or when you want a walk less strenuous than the norm. There are fifty of these routes (or areas) in all. The format used to describe these routes varies and depends on what is noteworthy; for example, the highest point is given for the walks which reach a comparatively high altitude, as this may be a factor on a day of low clouds.

The following notes clarify terms and conventions used in the route descriptions. A term such as "left (true) bank", used in reference to rivers or streams, means "the left bank as an observer faces downstream". A term such as "track/road" means that first a track and then a road is encountered. It does *not* mean that the route can be equally well described as a track or a road. The capital letter followed by six digits (or four if great precision is not needed) which is given with the starting point of each walk (and with a few other locations) is the grid reference of that point and uniquely identifies it on the map. The system is explained on nearly all maps.

For each route, except the easier routes, a distance and total climb is given and a total walking time based on Naismith's Rule (five kilometres per hour on the flat and 600 metres climbing per hour), as well as an additional time for exceptional difficulties in terrain. These difficulties are noted in the route descriptions, and an estimate of the additional time required is given after the walking time. The sum, therefore, of the standard Naismith's Rule time and the additional time for difficulties is an estimate of the total walking time. This estimate is undoubtedly extremely rough, as people vary greatly in their levels of fitness; what might slow down one person in certain conditions (for example, wet underfoot) might well be no bother to another. If nothing else, this total time gives an idea of the relative toughness of the walk.

These times are strictly walking duration, so unless you are a steady walker and do not stop to eat, look at the scenery or take photos, you will not complete the routes within the time suggested. Note also that if you are used to walking only on purposeful paths and tracks, you will find hill walking somewhat more difficult in Ireland where there are few.

MARATHON WALKS

. . . .

Within the text, I occasionally mention marathon walks. These are now a feature of hill walking in many countries. Each consists of a one-day long walk, and all are organised to the extent that they have check points, a mountain rescue service on the alert, and simple refreshments and first aid, if required. These walks are usually followed by social get-togethers for those who still have energy left after the day's exertions. Although the organisers of most of these walks suggest that participants have navigational skills, in practice endurance is more important.

Not all the marathon walks mentioned are necessarily organised every year and the routes and locations vary. In this book only the well-established walks are mentioned. The Mountaineering Council of Ireland will provide an up-to-date list.

TRANSPORT

....

The main sea-ports are Larne, Belfast, Dublin/Dun Laoghaire, Rosslare Harbour and Cork, the latter seasonal only. The main airports are at Dublin, Belfast, Shannon (near Limerick) and Cork, but there are also small airports at Knock (Mayo), Farranfore (Kerry), Galway, Sligo and Derry which are near mountains and may have regular services (you should check current schedule).

The express bus services radiate from Dublin and Belfast and there are trains to and from both cities. Details of express bus and rail services may be obtained by contacting the travel companies mentioned at the end of this book; there are brief outlines of relevant services given at appropriate points in the text.

By car

The road designation system in the Republic is M for motorways, N1-50 for national primary routes, N51-99 for national secondary routes and R for regional roads. Other minor roads are undesignated. The equivalent system in Northern Ireland is M, A, B and C.

The road system, North and South, is very dense and allows nearly all mountain areas to be readily accessed. However, quality does not always match quantity. The condition of roads in Northern Ireland is generally good. The Republic's roads are much poorer; on minor roads, plenty of time for travelling should be allowed. After you have sampled a few stretches of road of each designation, you will have a good idea of what to expect from others.

In the Republic, signposting on R-roads and minor roads, indicating areas of special interest to the hill walker, also contributes its share of woes. Firstly, some of the road signs still bear a superseded designation (T, L). Secondly, some distances are given in miles, others in kilometres, and it is not always clear which is meant. Worst of all, some signs have been turned on their posts, so that *all* signs are suspect. It is therefore advisable to use a map (the one you are using for walking will usually do) on R-roads and other minor roads and to check your position carefully. The details I give on how to find the start of routes may be of some help on the more convoluted minor roads.

By Bus

Local bus services are the ones which stop anywhere as long as it is safe to do so. Generally, the services are run by Irish Bus/Bus Eireann in the Republic, and Ulster Bus in Northern Ireland. The major exceptions are the north Donegal service which is run by the Lough Swilly Bus Co., and the service to Glendalough in Wicklow which is run by the St Kevin's Bus Service. Unfortunately, the head office of Irish Bus in Dublin does not have to hand out the exact routes of its services, so if you require detailed information, you must contact the regional offices.

The sketch maps show the approximate frequency of summer services on selected roads. (In this context, "frequency" refers to the number of bus journeys per week in either direction.) Remember that the service will not be quite so good in winter, and even in summer some services may be as infrequent as twice per week (once in each direction).

Notwithstanding these limitations, bus services are invaluable if you don't have a car, and even if you have they still greatly facilitate A to B walks. Given a choice, try to finish walks where there is a frequent service. It will be better for your peace of mind!

Hitch-hiking

Hitch-hiking is acceptable and common in country areas, especially as bus services are infrequent here. It is quite safe to do so, though women hitching alone, and particularly after dark, might be advised to use public transport.

ACCOMMODATION

A wide range of holiday accommodation from luxury hotels to hostels is available nearly everywhere in Ireland. *Guesthouse* accommodation can be obtained in nearly all towns and villages and in many rural areas. *Hostels*, both those belonging to the youth hostel associations and others, can be found in many places. *Self-catering* accommodation is fairly widespread. There are a number of adventure centres providing organised walking holidays, most of them in remote locations. Details of all these types of accommodation are given in the various publications issued by the two tourist organisations mentioned at the end of this book.

The sketch maps give the locations of the main tourist centres and hostels in or near the mountains. The up-to-date position of these hostels should be checked. In particular, note that not all accommodation is open for the entire year.

Lastly, camping. This is available at official sites and, if you politely ask the landowner's permission, in most upland areas of the country. Camping is not allowed in forest plantations or in national parks.

MAPS

. . . .

A country like Ireland which lacks a network of purposeful paths needs more than most a good set of small-scale maps for walkers. Although the maps of the Republic (not Northern Ireland, which are comprehensive) are at present still a rag-bag collection by most European standards, coverage of the mountain areas of the Republic is now quite good and improving, so that the gross deficiencies of the past are no longer such an obstacle to hill walkers. Maps available are:

1:250,000 (about a quarter inch to the mile) maps covering the whole island and useful for overall planning.

1:126,720 (half-inch to the mile) maps. The whole island (except the area round Belfast) is covered in a series published in the Republic. This scale is, of course, far too small for hill walking purposes. This is the only series available for most areas of the Republic, though most mountain areas are now covered on bigger scales. There is also a Northern Ireland series, better in terms of presentation, but now no longer published, though it is sometimes still available. It is worth noting that neither series makes a serious attempt to show cliffs comprehensively and that many minor roads are inaccurately depicted. The Republic's series shows forests very inadequately.

1:63,360 (one inch to the mile) maps. There are only three relevant Ordnance Survey maps: two for the Wicklow Mountains and one for Kerry. An old and out-of-date series, its only residual use is in covering areas not fully described by the 1:50,000 series. The maps have a contouring interval which is every one hundred feet to 1,000 feet, and 250 feet above that, so they give the impression that mountains level out in their higher slopes. They show cliffs, but very crudely and inaccurately.

The National Park authorities have produced *1:63,360 maps* for the national parks in Glenveagh (Donegal), Connemara and Killarney (Kerry). They cover only small areas and are on flimsy paper, but they are otherwise adequate – and inexpensive. As in other one-inch maps, the contouring is in feet.

1:50,000 (about one and a quarter inches to the mile) maps. Northern Ireland is covered in a colour-layered series with a ten-metre contour interval and cliffs indicated by symbols. Unfortunately, the contour lines are obscured by the colouring in some mountain areas. Most paths in mountain areas are depicted.

A set of *1:50,000 maps* is in the process of being published for the Republic, with most mountain areas now covered. In its initial few years the series has undergone a metamorphosis. After a period during which the sheets were designated as "Preliminary First Series" and in a few cases "Rambler", the later maps are now designated "Discovery Series" and are easily recognised by their purple covers. The presentation in the "Discovery Series" maps is much better, but the most important single difference between the earlier maps and the "Discovery Series" is that the former are uncoloured and the latter discreetly layer-coloured. The earlier maps should be treated with some caution as they have a considerable number of errors, though the contouring is accurate. Specific errors in these (and all other maps) are noted at appropriate points in the text.

Since these Republic of Ireland 1:50,000 maps are the ones which will be used by hill walkers in most parts of the country, it might be helpful to point out some of their idiosyncrasies in a little detail:

● cliffs are generally depicted by the convergence of contour lines and not outlined explicitly;

● paths are generally not shown, except for the long-distance paths; however, they are generally of a haphazard nature and therefore difficult to depict;

● many areas of forest are shown high on mountain sides, which is in fact open country; if the forestry plantation you have been looking out for does not materialise, it may be that it simply does not exist;

● the thin, black irregular lines in some upland areas are boundary markers, in most instances walls; they are not explained in the legend.

In addition to the series produced by the Ordnance Survey, a commercial enterprise has published an excellent 1:50,000 map of Connemara with a thirty-metre contour interval. This map shows cliffs explicitly and accurately.

1:25,000 (about two and a half inches to the mile) maps. This scale is probably too large for the average hill walker; the frequent refolding necessary under sometimes adverse mountain conditions makes these maps awkward to use. The

Mournes are covered on one map and there are two for the main mountain area of Kerry. The maps of Kerry do not give much more information than the 1:50,000 maps covering the same area, so they may be considered a doubtful investment. All the above 1:25,000 maps have a ten-metre contouring interval.

The Comeraghs, a small range in the South-East region, is covered by a 1:25,000 map with a five-metre contouring interval. Unfortunately, it is rather expensive.

The National Park authorities have produced a 1:25,000 map of the Glendalough (Wicklow) area. It is in the same style as the other national park maps described above, except that the contouring is metric at a fifteen-metre interval.

To summarise the above, the following regions and ranges are well-mapped at present: the Comeraghs and Slieve Blooms in the South-East region; most of the Wicklow region; Northern Ireland; Donegal; nearly all the North Connaught region; most of the Mayo region; Connemara; most of the Kerry region.

The following regions and areas are not well-mapped at present: the Galtees, the Knockmealdowns, the Blackstairs and some minor ranges in the South-East region, in effect nearly all this region; the northern and southern ends of the Wicklow region; part of the Mayo region; the south and parts of the east of the Kerry region.

The maps covering each range are indicated in the text and the extent of each in the sketch maps. The half-inch (1:126,720) maps, as they cover the whole island, are not shown on the sketch maps.

Finally, an obvious question is: which map should be used with each route described in this book? It is important to emphasise that a map must be used in conjunction with the brief route descriptions given, except for some of the easier routes where the fact that no map is needed is specifically mentioned.

The best map available at the time of writing (early 1994) is the one mentioned at the start of each route description, that is, the reference map. The topographical names used in the route description are the same as those used on the reference map; if a feature is not named on that map, it is linked in some other way to the map (for example, grid reference, spot height).

If you haven't got the reference map, an alternative (usually the Ordnance Survey half-inch map) will usually suffice; just to be sure, the route should nonetheless be carefully traced out beforehand, so that you know exactly what the itinerary is.

It may be that a better map than the reference map will be available when you come to walk some of the routes. This map will be one in the "Discovery Series", replacing another in the 1:50,000 series, or replacing a half-inch map. Given a choice, by all means buy the new and better map, even though it is not the reference one.

SAFETY

. . . .

Continental visitors will be surprised by how remote and demanding Irish mountains that are only 500 metres high are. Both continental and British visitors will be surprised by the absence of other walkers and of paths. Irish mountains should therefore be treated with the respect due to continental mountains several times higher. These conditions demand greater proficiency in the use of map and compasss, and hill walkers should be aware that if an accident occurs it may be difficult to get help quickly. The absence of good maps in some areas of the Republic is another factor which hill walkers should keep in mind. It is therefore important that the following guidelines should be adhered to carefully.

Don't walk alone. For more difficult walks, three is the recommended minimum, and four better. Let someone know where you are going to be. Don't be over-ambitious. If you are inexperienced or unused to Irish mountain conditions, choose an easier route. Dress for the occasion. Boots with ankle support are highly desirable if not essential for all the one-day walks given in this book. Take a cagoule and make sure that you have sufficient warm, waterproof clothing as weather conditions can change rapidly and unexpectedly. Carry sufficient food, including a hot drink. Carry all your gear in a rucksack and, even taking into account the provisions you need, do not be weighed down with unnecessary gear. Take a map and compass and, most importantly, know how to use them. Don't carry on with the planned route if worsening weather or oncoming nightfall suggest a prudent retreat.

If the worst comes to the worst and there is an accident, keep the patient warm and comfortable, note the exact position, leave someone with the patient and send a competent person for help. The mountain rescue may be alerted by ringing 999.

In general, use a modicum of common sense, take reasonable precautions and then – without being overawed by the dangers – enjoy yourself.

THE BEST TIME OF YEAR

. . . .

It hardly needs saying that weather is the most important factor to get right when walking in Ireland and that it is the one completely in the lap of the gods. Since millions of words have been expended on this subject to no discernible effect, I do not propose to add many more. The truest and most useless generalisation is that you can get good weather – and bad – at any time of year.

First, rain. Just to confirm your worst suspicions, records show 225 wet days per year in the mountains of the west and 175 in the mountains elsewhere. Rain and low cloud that come with warm fronts are the greatest bane of the hill walker. By contrast, cold fronts bring showers and bright, clear periods and are much more acceptable.

April, May and June tend to be the driest months in most parts of the country and these months, as well as September and early October, are probably the best for walking. July and August tend to be a bit warm and humid, with poor visibility. (In addition, at this time of year accommodation is likely to be crowded.) The months of November to March are rainy (with the west having a pronounced and high winter maximum) and the days short. Generally, winter is not very inviting, though occasionally there are cold, fresh days with bright sun that can be delightful. Snow, which is fairly infrequent, does not lie long. It is more prevalent in the east than the west.

Little need be said about the wind except that it is generally stronger in the west and that since westerlies prevail, try to walk west to east (that is, with it on your back) on higher ground. Vegetation, of which bracken is the most unpleasant, is, of course, at its highest in late summer. In particular, it infests ground close to river banks and areas directly above enclosed fields. Midges, the scourge of the summer hill walker in Scotland, are not so prevalent in Ireland.

THE SOUTH-EAST

. . . .

There was one particularly fine view over the inset Loch
Muskry (a classic armchair corrie complete with water
cushion) along to the cone of Galtymore. O'Loughman's
Castle was very clear: a squat, square, crenellated tower
until it is approached off Greenane when it disintegrates,
as if by magic, into a crumbly conglomerate outcrop.
It *must* be a place of legends . . .

Hamish Brown,
Hamish's Groats End Walk, 1981

. . . . .

The small mountain ranges of the South-East are with one
exception composed of either old red sandstone or Silurian
rock. They are somewhat subdued in form but nonetheless
surprisingly high, and boast one of Ireland's few Munros (peaks
over 914 metres/3,000 feet high). Unusually for Ireland, all
the ranges are outside the ambience of the sea: they mostly
rise from rich, well-populated, cultivated land and wide,
coniferous plantations. One other general point: the Galtees,
Knockmealdowns and the Comeraghs are quite close to each
other, none too demanding and have plenty of varied accommodation around them. For these reasons they lend themselves
to an easy week-long walking tour, though the absence of good
maps (see below) makes accurate planning difficult.

The *Galtees* (routes 1 to 3, 10) are a range twenty-five
kilometres/fifteen miles long with a simple structure. The

broad, gently sloped spine of the range runs east-west, culminating in Galtymore at 919 metres/3,018 feet. This is the only Munro, though the average height of the range is quite impressive. The western two-thirds of the range is the more interesting, with navigation greatly helped by an upland wall that runs along part of the main ridge. Further east the range tends towards bland, gentle mounds. The views from the tops of the entire range are particularly extensive, though not spectacular, and cover an expanse of lowland to the north and the Knockmealdowns, and farther away a glimpse of the sea to the south.

North of the spine are a series of fine, grassy, high-walled corries, three of which carry lakes. These northern slopes are extensively forested. The southern slopes are also much forested, though the gradient is gentler. Tiny, partly wooded glens (in their higher reaches no more than grassy ravines) add greatly to the attraction of this side. Access from the south is by lengthy ascents on rough roads. Unfortunately, the mapping of the Galtees is particularly poor.

A marathon west-east walk along the Galtees is organised for August of each year.

The *Knockmealdowns* (routes 4, 5) are similar to the Galtees; they consist of a simple east-west ridge about twenty-five kilometres/fifteen miles long with the northern slopes considerably steeper than the southern. However, they are less dramatic than the Galtees; there is but one corrie lake and no well-formed corries. The highest peak, also called Knockmealdown, at 795 metres/2,609 feet is 120 metres/400 feet lower than Galtymore and lies in the generally higher and more rugged eastern section of the range. The northern slopes in particular are highly afforested, so access is restricted in many places, with problems made worse by the out-of-date depiction of minor roads on the maps. Three motorable north-south roads, one of which is the well-surfaced scenic Vee Road [R668] cross the range. They provide an excellent means of access but mostly only for there-and-back walks, unless a second car is parked at the top of a neighbouring pass to allow an A to B walk.

The *Comeraghs* (routes 6, 7, 11, 12) and their southward extension, the Monavullaghs, extend south from the town of Clonmel in a zigzag fashion. The range is easily accessible from the west on a road which continues as a bridle path through the range. North of the path a long, narrow ridge with bold conglomerate tors extends to the very north of the range, in which the highest peak is Knockanaffrin (755 metres/2,478 feet). South of the path, peaks barely rise from a wet peat-hagged plateau, but this central section (central, that is, if the Monavullaghs are considered part of the range) is almost ringed by a set of fine corries containing beautiful lakes. One of these, the easily accessible Coumshingaun, is generally considered the finest corrie in the country. Just behind the corrie is the highest peak in the range, the nondescript Fauscoum (792 metres/2,597 feet), which barely rises above the general level of the plateau. A marathon walk, the "Comeragh Bog Trot" (mercifully it does not quite live up to its name) is organised for April of every year.

The *Monavullaghs* are at the southern end of the Comeragh chain. Though they are considered drier and less boggy than the rest of the range, this does not fully compensate for the absence of the corries which are the prime attraction of the more northerly part of the range.

The Comeraghs (including the Monavullaghs) are mapped

at 1:50,000, a distinction in a region that is generally poorly mapped.

Geologically a part of the granite Leinster Chain, the *Blackstairs* (routes 8, 13) are shaped like a rough F, their main ridge extending north-south, high in the north at mast-topped Mount Leinster (796 metres/2,610 feet) and petering out in the south. The range is composed of heathery, gently sloped mountains, nowhere more than one mountain wide. There are no cliffs, corries or mountain lakes. A road crosses the range at Sculloge Gap south of Mount Leinster, and the area south of this, a grassy ridge with some fine tors, is the most scenic and commands long views. A comparatively easy marathon walk is organised in May every year along the main chain of the Blackstairs.

The *Slieve Blooms* (routes 9, 14) are as near the centre of Ireland as any mountain group, so that in good visibility the views from parts of the tops are very wide. Unfortunately, the tops are otherwise of little interest: rolling bogland reaching a height of 506 metres/1,660 feet. The surrounding valleys, through which the waymarked Slieve Bloom Way threads, offer some pleasant walking, though extensive forestry plantations do not improve their attractiveness. Given that there is a modern 1:50,000 map and that facilities in the form of picnic tables are excellent, it is a pity to have to say that the Slieve Blooms are worth a visit only as a break on the way to somewhere else.

Lastly in this region we should mention the groups of small and generally subdued and gently sloped hills of north County Tipperary and north County Cork. The Silvermine Mountains of north Tipperary are not very exciting but the Devil's Bit (bite) to their east are indented by a great glacial spillway, a dramatic feature as seen from the N7 (Dublin-Limerick road). The four small ranges of north Cork are centred on the town of Mallow and offer undemanding walking, though one of them, the Boggeraghs, rises as high as 646 metres/2,118 feet.

Access: access to the region is good, with adequate road and rail connections. Cahir, Clonmel, Carrick-on-Suir, Portlaoise (for the Slieve Blooms) and Enniscorthy (for the Blackstairs) have rail stations. The express bus service to (and through) the region is quite good. Clonmel is about 130 kilometres/eighty miles from Rosslare Harbour and 170 kilometres/105 miles from Dublin.

Roads and accommodation: the road system within the region is good and no mountain range is hard to reach. Finding the start of walks in the maze of side roads to be negotiated after leaving the main roads is likely to be the principal difficulty for the traveller by car. There are many good centres close to each of the ranges, with Clonmel in particular well placed for the Galtees, Knockmealdowns and Comeraghs, and Clogheen well placed for the Galtees and Knockmealdowns.

Local bus services: these tend to run parallel to the ranges rather than over them. There is, however, an infrequent service close to the Comeraghs and Knockmealdowns at Ballymacarbery and several, some express, close to the Blackstairs at Kiltealy.

Maps: the Comeraghs are covered on Discovery Series sheet 75, and this range also has a privately produced 1:25,000 map, but it is rather expensive and therefore not given here as a reference map. The Slieve Blooms are covered by sheet 54, which is one of the first in the modern 1:50,000 series and probably the most unreliable.

Coverage of the remainder of the region is only at half-inch

(1:126,720). Blind faith in the accuracy of minor roads depicted on these maps in any part of the region is inadvisable. The Knockmealdowns are on one map (sheet 22), as are the Blackstairs (sheet 19). But pity the walker in the Galtees! This range is on two half-inch sheets (18, 22) with the edge of each sheet running along the spine of the range (and there is no overlap between sheets). This gives the Galtees the unenviable reputation of being the worst-mapped range in the country.

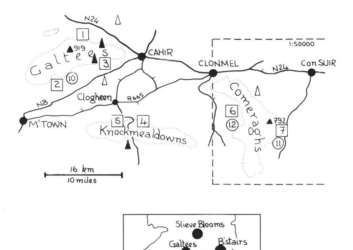

Route 1: Galtees – Galtymore

Maps 18 and 22 (half-inch).

Drive 1.7 miles west of Condon's Pub to junction of minor road running south off Glen of Aherlow Road and just west of bridge (R 871281). Cross to east of bridge, take first tarmac road south to end of forest on left, ascend Cush initially on rough path, take ridge to Galtybeg (detour to O'Loughman's Castle adds four kilometres, climb 240 metres), climb Galtymore (cross, trig pillar), then follow wall that begins on west side of summit, leaving it to descend spur on west side of Lough Curra. Follow earthbank running north on east side of this spur to reach south end of track, and take track downhill to start.

Distance: 13 kilometres.   Climb: 1,050 metres.

Time: 4.5 hours.

Route 2: West Galtees

Map 22 (half-inch).

Start at end of tarmac (R 868197), reached by taking turn north off N8, 0.8 miles east of Kilbeheny, and forking right after further 1.2 miles. Walk track north to Monabrack, follow spur to Carrignabinnia (detour to Galtymore adds six kilometres, climb 350 metres). Keep steep ground on right to follow wall to Lyracappul (wall ends here), climb Temple Hill (large cairn, trig pillar), descend south-east to reach stream and follow it to end of tarmac near confluence of streams (shown on map). Walk tarmac south-east about 500 metres, then ascend spur on left to grassy track near crest of spur. Walk tracks to nearby start.

Distance: 12 kilometres.   Climb: 800 metres.

Time: 3.75 hours.

Route 3: East Galtees

Map 22 (half-inch).

Start at Mountain Lodge Youth Hostel (R 919210). Take forest track north-west on east of stream. At forest end after two kilometres, walk west to cross two streams and then pick up intermittent track to col north of Knockeenatoung. Join better track (the "Black Road") running initially north then north-west to col between Galtymore and Galtybeg; climb Galtybeg. Walk east to O'Loughman's Castle (prominent tor), descend to col towards Greenane, walk south-west to forest edge to join outward track.

> Distance: 13 kilometres.   Climb: 700 metres.
> Time: 3.75 hours.

Route 4: East Knockmealdowns

Map 22 (half-inch).

Start at car park at signposted Liam Lynch monument (S 096112), reached by driving south from Goatenbridge/ Goat's Bridge. Walk towards monument and take firebreak right to open ground. Climb Crohan West, Knockmeal, Knocknafallia, Knocknagnauv, Knockmealdown (trig pillar) – avoid corrie to north-east of latter. (Detour to Sugar Loaf Hill and contour back adds five kilometres, climb one hundred metres – this is one of the most scenic parts of the range.) Walk spur north to point 2,521 feet and then descend directly east (thus avoiding forest to north) to walk track along left bank of Glengalla River. At end of track cross two adjacent streams to east, thereby reaching main track running north. Follow forest tracks, signposted to monument, to reach start.

An intermittent bank or wall which runs from Crohan west to Knockmeal and then follows the county boundary west (and therefore not necessarily over all the peaks) is helpful to navigation.

Distance: 16 kilometres.   Climb: 850 metres.
Time: 4.75 hours.

Route 5: West Knockmealdowns

Map 22 (half-inch); this map is very inaccurate in its depiction of roads to north of route, so it should not be relied upon as west-to-east finish of walk.

Start at car park at junction of minor road and R668 (S 027114). Take path south past Bay Lough to R668 at the Gap. Walk main ridge west following intermittent bank to point circa 2,000 feet, then walk to Knockshanahullion (large cairn, trig pillar), descend north to contour on intermittent track and path along south of forest as far as Bay Lough. Retrace path to start.

Distance: 10 kilometres.   Climb: 700 metres.
Time: 3.25 hours.

Route 6: North Comeraghs

Map 75 (1:50,000), Discovery Series.

Start at car park (S 276128). Walk back along road, turning

right just before church. Walk road to end and continue straight ahead on track into open country, initially following stream, to Knocksheegowna (outcrops, trig pillar). Walk ridge south-east over Knockanaffrin to the the Gap. Path to start.

Distance: 16 kilometres.   Climb: 650 metres.
Time: 4.5 hours.

Route 7: Comeraghs – Coumshingaun

Map 75 (1:50,000), Discovery Series.

Start at Kilclooney Bridge on R676 (S 349116). Take side road/path west to corrie lake of Coumshingaun and ascend south arm of corrie (some mild scrambling near top) to reach plateau near Fauscoum (point 792 metres). Descend north arm of corrie to lake, retrace steps to start. Route may easily be extended to take in rims of corries to west and north, but note much featureless terrain.

Distance: 8 kilometres.   Climb: 700 metres.
Time: 2.75 hours.

Route 8: South Blackstairs

Map 19 (half-inch); this map is inaccurate in its depiction of roads in the area.

Start on minor road (S 792451). To get there, take road signposted "Glynn" from Ballymurphy for 0.8 miles, turn left

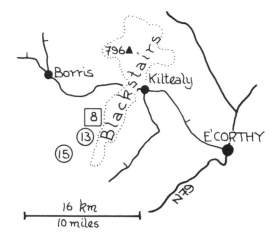

here, drive for further one mile and park at the right-angle bend. Walk south to cross nearby gate on left just before first farmhouse on right, walk initially indistinct track roughly south to col north-east of Carrigalachan. Climb Caher Roe's Den, point 2,409 feet, walk along its north spur to descend northwest through fields to road at about S 810478. Turn left, walk along road for two kilometres to crest of low hill; take very narrow road here on left through Walshstown, turn left at tee for start.

> Distance: 13 kilometres. Climb: 650 metres.
> Time: 3.75 hours.

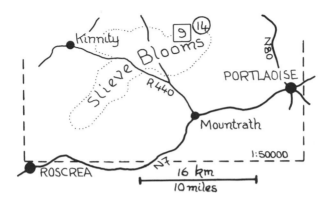

Route 9: Slieve Blooms

Map 54 (1:50,000), preliminary edition; this edition shows the
Slieve Bloom Way in places traversing trackless country where
it is in fact on forest tracks.

Start at Glenbarrow car park off R422 (S 368082). Take Slieve
Bloom Way down to nearby river and continue on track (not
shown on map) and road to the Cut (a high point on minor
road crossing range). Turn left here to climb Barna,
Baunreaghcong, Carnahinch. Walk north-east to rejoin Way
at large cairn, then follow rough path whose route is indicated
by tall poles across some wet terrain. Forest tracks, still on
way, to end.

Distance: 20 kilometres.   Climb: 400 metres.
Time: 4.75 hours.

Easier Routes in the South-East

Route 10

Map 22 (half-inch).

The narrow glens at the west end of the south side of the Galtees, reached by the road described in route 2 or by parallel roads further east (for example, the road leading off N8, 3.2 miles east of Kilbeheny).

Route 11

No map needed.

Coumshingaun corrie lake, reached as in the start of route 7.

Route 12

No map needed.

The corries on the west side of the Comeraghs, reached from the starting point of route 6.

Route 13

Map 19 (half-inch).

The south end of the Blackstairs using the start of route 8 and walking south on the main ridge, returning by same route.

Route 14

Map 54 (1:50,000).

Glenbarrow in the Slieve Blooms (start of route 9), but leaving the Slieve Bloom Way to continue north-east on tracks; reach a minor road at N 356097 (where road running north-west is not shown on map).

Route 15

Map 19 (half-inch).

Brandon Hill (S 6940) from the north-west, starting from end of laneway off the Inistioge – Graignamanagh road and 1.6 miles along this road from the Graignamanagh direction. Highest point: 520 metres.

Further Reading about the South-East

East and South: New Irish Walk Guides, by David Herman and Miriam Joyce McCarthy (Gill and Macmillan, 1991). Thirty-five of the walks in the book cover this region.

WICKLOW

. . . .

At Glendalough, there is a noble CASCADE; the Lake thereof, is bounded on three Sides by vast, high and almost inaccessible mountains, that on the west Side is of a prodigeous height. Through the middle part there glides a smart River, from one Rock to another, descending nearly a mile before it enters the Lake at the Foot of the Mountain . . . but what is surprising, the Natives affirm, that it passes through that Lake without mixing with its waters.

James Weeks, *A New Geography of Ireland,* 1752

. . . . .

This region of granitic mountains stretches in a long (fifty kilometres, thirty miles), broad line south-west from the outskirts of Dublin. As such it is the largest area of upland in Ireland and encompasses much fine walking country, part of it attractively remote, though other parts are gently shelving and bleak. It is particularly suited for long, but not over-strenuous walks. As an indication of its importance as a high amenity area close to a major city, some of the eastern side of the range is now in the Wicklow Mountains National Park and it is planned that more will be in the future. The popular Wicklow Way runs south from Dublin through a long stretch of this eastern side. Animal lovers – and others – will be impressed by the herds of deer, mostly sika and hybrids of sika and red deer, which roam the entire upland area.

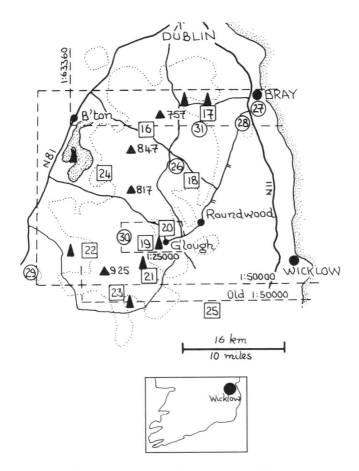

Of course, there are problems. In spite of its extent, access to open mountain is restricted in some, though only some, places. Forestry covers parts of several mountain valleys and even extends high into the hills; forestry tracks, though plentiful, are not routed to facilitate access. Near Dublin, farmland

45

may also block access. In this area farmers have suffered constant trespass and so do not welcome walkers, well-intentioned or not. This is therefore an area where guidebooks are particularly useful to avoid access difficulties.

Not entirely unrelated to its proximity to Dublin, walkers should not leave valuables in their cars. In recent years there has been a constant stream of break-ins to unattended cars in remote, and not so remote areas of the mountains.

There are two marathon walks in the Wicklow Mountains. The Lug Walk, at fifty-three kilometres/thirty-three miles, is the longest but not the toughest marathon in Ireland; it takes place in June of every odd-numbered year. On even-numbered years the somewhat shorter Glen of Imaal marathon takes place in the south-west of the region.

In the very north, the mountains of County Dublin bear much evidence of the city's proximity in the form of masts, littering and eroded paths. Though broken by some pleasant glacial valleys and with hills rising gently to a considerable 757 metres/2,475 feet at Kippure (route 16), this northern end is mostly a plateau or shelving moorland. In contrast, close to the city (and the sea) are Bray Head and the Sugar Loafs (routes 27, 28); they are low (Great Sugar Loaf rises to only 501 metres/1,654 feet) but craggy and give short but energetic strolls.

South of Kippure the granitic north-east to south-west spine is more evident. The three highest mountains in the range lie along it, all three sheltering high, attractive corries. These peaks are Mullaghcleevaun (847 metres/2,688 feet), which is connected southward to Tonelagee (817 metres/2,686 feet) by high-level moorland, south of which is Lugnaquillia (925 metres/3,039 feet), the only Munro in the range. The moorland south of Mullaghcleevaun is exceptionally wet and in parts riven by deep gullies interspersed by peat hags, the latter a feature of much of the lower-lying areas between the hills in this entire range. South of Lugnaquillia the general height is much lower, with pleasant, quiet, wooded valleys interspersed between the higher ground (routes 23, 25).

East of the central spine are a series of fine, steep-sided glacial valleys of which the best-known is Glendalough, an important medieval monastic settlement. Other valleys, especially Glenmalure, are equally attractive. The most satisfying routes in the region are probably those taking in the rugged peaks on this side of the range: Djouce, Fancy, Scarr, the eastern side of Tonelagee or Croaghan Moira (routes 17 to 21, 30, 31).

West of the central spine, wide river valleys and extensively forested moorland on gently sloping hills predominate, with the extensive Pollaphuca Reservoir mitigating its austerity (routes 22, 24, 29). The broad Glen of Imaal in the south is almost surrounded by a fine circuit of hills; unfortunately, much of its eastern side is out-of-bounds as it is an artillery range.

Lugnaquillia itself, at the southern end of the central spine, is the centre of a starfish-like set of high-level spurs. Its grassy summit plateau, topped by a huge cairn, provides the climax to several good circuits, which can start from almost any direction (routes 21 to 23).

Access: access to the area is excellent as it lies adjacent to major ports, particularly Dublin. Glendalough in the heart of the mountains is about fifty kilometres/thirty miles from Dublin and one hundred kilometres/sixty miles from Rosslare Harbour. Express bus services run parallel to the spine of the range along the N11 and N81, through rather distant from it. The rail links are not very convenient.

Roads and accommodation: the road system is generally good. A road (the Military Road) runs parallel and close to the spine of the range and provides an excellent drive. Two high-level east-west roads cross the range. These three roads give a good introduction to the range and provide starting points for walks.

Logistically, Dublin, the hub of the transport systems and with varied accommodation, is the best centre, but if you dislike cities, there are several good smaller centres, though none equally well located as Dublin for the east and west of the range. Of these Glendalough is easily accessible and is well placed in a lovely location. Other good centres are Roundwood or Enniskerry on the east, and Blessington or Baltinglass on the west. There is a good choice of youth hostels, some of which are within walking distance of one another, so that a hostel-to-hostel walking trip is feasible.

Local bus services: parts of the range, especially the northern fringe and the Glen of Imaal, are well served by Dublin Bus. The St Kevin's Bus Service provides an invaluable service to Glendalough.

Maps: the maps covering the region are quite a motley collection. A good Discovery Series 1:50,000 map (sheet 56) covers the bulk of the mountains. Parts of the north and south are covered by old one-inch (1:63,360) maps ("District" series). An old and execrable 1:50,000 map (the "Wicklow Way"), now out of print but possibly still available at some outlets, covers some of the south. It is marginally useful for some areas not covered by other maps. Two sheets of the half-inch series (16, 19) also cover the mountains, the bulk on the former. The route of the Wicklow Way is covered by a map/guide at a scale of 1:50,000 (see Further Reading about Wicklow, below).

A 1:25,000 map covering the area around Glendalough is issued by the National Park authorities. It shows paths and tracks in great detail, though the present edition (1988) depicts an out-of-date route for the Wicklow Way.

Note that on the accompanying sketch map the coverage of the "old 1:50,000" map is not shown in the area that is better covered by sheet 56. The Wicklow District map runs only three kilometres south of sheet 56 and is therefore not shown at all on the sketch map.

Route 16: North Wicklow – Kippure

Map 56 (1:50,000), Discovery Series.

Start at forest car park (not signposted prominently) on north side of R759 at O 080145. Follow left (true) bank of stream, and beyond climb to Seefingan (724 metres, megalithic tomb). Following intermittent ditch through much wet ground, walk to Kippure (TV mast) and then descend south to bridge on R759 at O 110127. Cross road and follow river downstream to bridge on left. Here walk to road on right and take it to start.

> Distance: 13 kilometres.   Climb: 550 metres.
> Time: 3.5 hours.

Route 17: North-East Wicklow – Djouce

Map 56 (1:50,000), Discovery Series.

Start at Crone car park on south side of Glencree at O 192143.

Follow Wicklow Way south to col one kilometre south of Djouce; climb Djouce (rocky outcrops, trig pillar) following fence posts. Continue along fence posts, passing coffin-shaped stone, to col south of War Hill. Climb War Hill (indistinct summit), descend north to cross valley and ascend to col west of Maulin. Climb Maulin. Descend north to south-west corner of forest and follow forest paths/tracks downhill to start.

Distance: 13 kilometres.   Climb: 650 metres.
Time: 3.75 hours.

Route 18: East Wicklow

Map 56 (1:50,000), Discovery Series.

Start at large gate pillars on south-west side of R759 (O 172064). Take tarmac, later track/path to north shore of Lough Dan, climb north to Knocknacloghoge (534 metres), cross Cloghoge Brook (detour left may be necessary after rain), climb Fancy (595 metres, indistinct summit, no cairn), descend south-east with cliffs initially on left to reach side track close to confluence of Cloghoge Brook with Cloghoge River; retrace initial steps.

Distance: 12 kilometres.   Climb: 750 metres.
Time: 3.75 hours.

Route 19: East Wicklow – Glendalough

Map 56 (1:50,000), Discovery Series.

Start at upper car park Glendalough (T 111964). Ascend steep path north, then west to climb Camaderry (two summits) and pass south of reservoir. Walk to Lough Firrib along intermittent trench (careful navigation required!), then south-west to Conavalla, or in good visibility nearby point 702 metres (escape is possible on this leg). Keep to high ground to south-east on intermittent path and track (Lugduff, 652 metres, has white quartzite rocks on summit), walk on path with cliffs on left along spur running west to east on south side of Glendalough Upper Lake. At steep drop ahead near east end of lake, cross stile right to reach forest track. Take track/path to start, with waterfall on right.

Distance: 18 kilometres.   Climb: 700 metres.
Time: 4.75 hours.

Route 20: East Wicklow – Glenmacnass

Map 56 (1:50,000), Discovery Series.

Start at Laragh (T 142996). Take Wicklow Way north to Paddock Hill, climb Scarr (641 metres), descend north-west, passing standing stone, then west to car park at O 116029 (escape possible here). Cross river on natural stepping stones about seventy metres upstream, climb south arm of corrie containing Lough Ouler to reach Tonelagee (trig pillar). Descend south-east and follow indeterminate tops generally south-east (careful navigation on undulating ground) to point 470 metres. From here take spur south, veering immediately east off it to descend through gap between larch stands. Follow forest tracks and Wicklow Way to start (complicated track network at end, so National Park 1:25,000 map might be reassuring).

Distance: 20 kilometres.   Climb: 1,100 metres.
Time: 6 hours.

Route 21: East Wicklow – Lugnaquillia

Map 56 (1:50,000), Discovery Series.

Start at car park at head of Glenmalure (T 066943). Cross footbridge and take partially concealed path immediately opposite to meet forest track. Turn left and cross river where track swings sharply right at fork. Keep between fence and river at first to climb Lugnaquillia (large cairn, trig pillar). Walk east to Clohernagh (indistinct summit), avoiding cliffs on right at first and keeping left at cairn marking fork of spurs. Descend east from Clohernagh, picking up path with cliffs on left. Continue east (no path) to reach top of grassy zigzag track and descend into Glenmalure, crossing footbridge to reach road. Walk road three kilometres to start.

Distance: 15 kilometres.   Climb: 800 metres.
Time: 4.5 hours.

Route 22: West Wicklow – Lugnaquillia

Map 56 (1:50,000), Discovery Series.

Start at road junction in Glen of Imaal (S 983948). Walk road south-west to Seskin (S 973935) and then east to foot of Camara

Hill. Climb Camara Hill, initially following army waymarks; climb Lugnaquillia, walk 300 metres north-east to avoid cliffs, then follow high ground to Camenabologue, taking care not to take spurs east on this leg. Walk one kilometre north to pass and descend west on path following army waymarks to start.

Careful! Army range in vicinity. Warning flags fly occasionally – if so, do not walk route. If in doubt, consult army by ringing 045-54626.

Distance: 19 kilometres.   Climb: 900 metres.
Time: 5.5 hours.

Route 23: South Wicklow – Lugnaquillia

"Wicklow Way" map (1:50,000) or map 16 (half-inch).

Start at Aghavannagh Youth Hostel (T 059860). Walk one kilometre west along road, cross gate right at junction left. Walk track to first farmhouse, turn left here to cross gate and continue, initially on track to climb Lybagh, Slievemaan (both indistinct summits) Lugnaquillia. Initially keeping clear of cliffs on right, walk east to cairn marking junction of spurs, then walk south-east to Corrigasleggaun (point 2,534 feet, indistinct summit). Keep to high ground by walking south then south-east, veering left off spur (called Doyle Street on "Wicklow Way"map) to meet forest track at about T 060895. Follow this track (initially south-east) for about 3.5 kilometres to sharp right turn just before prominent bridge (both maps are inaccurate in their depiction of forest tracks in this area). Take this right turn to reach road.

> Distance: 18 kilometres.   Climb: 750 metres.
> Time: 5 hours.

Route 24: West Wicklow – Mullaghcleevaun

Map 56 (1:50,000), Discovery Series. Map exaggerates extent of forest at start.

Start at bridge in hamlet of Glenbride (O 037043). To get there, drive 0.4 miles west of Ballinagee Bridge on R756, turn north, take first right off this road. Cross bridge westward, then take first gate right into forest. Walk north-west to top of forest and follow fence to near top of Silsean (698 metres, indistinct summit). Continue through pathless moorland to Moanbane (indistinct summit), Mullaghcleevaun (trig pillar, memorial). Descend south-west spur (boggy terrain, take care not to take spur south-east) to Glasnagollum Brook and cross valley to start.

> Distance: 12 kilometres.   Climb: 650 metres.
> Time: 3.5 hours.

Route 25: South Wicklow

Map 19 (half-inch).

Start at track off minor road (T 104744). To get there from Aughrim, drive R747 for 2.5 miles, turn left (signposted "Toberpatrick"), turn left at T-junction. Turn first right and park at second turn right, a track running north-east. Take this track; at nearby T-junction, cross field ahead and climb north-west spur of Croghan Mountain to summit (small trig pillar), partly on track. Walk north-east with block of forest on right and later with another block of forest on left to reach Ballinasilloge. Retrace steps to south end of last block of forest encountered and descend west, then contour west to reach track.

Distance: 13 kilometres.   Climb: 500 metres.
Time: 3.5 hours.

Easier Routes in Wicklow

Route 26

Map 56 (1:50,000) hardly needed.

The Lough Dan/Lough Tay area, starting at the same point as route 18.

Route 27

Map 56 (1:50,000) hardly needed.

Bray Head (north and south tops) from Bray (O 2717), returning directly from south top to reach sea-cliff path.

Route 28

Map 56 (1:50,000).

Great Sugar Loaf from Kilmacanoge (O 2414), approached on side roads and rough tracks (route initially parallel to R755).

Route 29

Map 16 (half-inch).

Brusselstown Ring approached from the road junction at S 901943 and returning by side roads to south.

Route 30

National Park map (1:25,000).

Glenealo Valley from car park at Upper Lake, Glendalough (T 111964). Other routes can be easily found in this area, facilitated by National Park 1:25,000 map.

Route 31

Map 56 (1:50,000).

From Crone car park (O 193143) along the Wicklow Way to near Powerscourt Waterfall, crossing the east shoulder of Maulin and returning by contouring west along its north side to south-west corner of forest. Here follow end of route 17. Highest point: 450 metres.

Further Reading about Wicklow

East and South: New Irish Walk Guides, by David Herman and Miriam Joyce McCarthy (Gill and Macmillan, 1991). Thirty-two of the walks in the book cover this region.

The Wicklow Way from Marley to Glenmalure, by Michael Fewer (Gill and Macmillan, 1988). Route description of the northern part of the Way, with background notes.

The Wicklow Way, by J.B. Malone (O'Brien Press, updated 1993). Detailed route description.

Hill Strollers' Wicklow, by David Herman (Shanksmare, new edition 1994). Thirty-five detailed descriptions of shorter walks.

Hill Walkers' Wicklow, by David Herman (Shanksmare, new edition 1993). Twenty-four detailed descriptions of longer walks.

On Foot in Dublin and Wicklow, by Christopher Moriarty (Wolfhound). Forty-six easy strolls, some in mountain areas, with emphasis on flora and fauna.

Access Routes, by the Irish Ramblers Club (new edition 1988). Short routes to reach open country in the Wicklow Mountains.

The Wicklow Way, The Map Guide for Walkers (EastWest Mapping, 1993).

NORTHERN IRELAND

I looked across the glen below the ridge of Bearnagh
to the opposite slopes of Slieve Meel-More, all veiled
in the cloud. On that cloud I first saw a small circular
rainbow, and then with the sun gaining strength, at my
back, the full Broken spectre; myself leaning on the wall
encircled by concentric rainbows and projected across
the valley on to the wall of mist. This is the famous
spectre named from the Broken in Germany
from which it was first described, the magnified shadow
flung across a deep valley.

> D.C.C. Pochin Mould,
> *The Mountains of Ireland,* 1976

. . . . .

It must be conceded that Northern Ireland does not hang
together as a natural unit for the purposes of this book – nor
can it simply be tagged onto other regions. What the mountain
ranges in Northern Ireland have in common arises from a
separate administration: a better map coverage, better roads
and signposting and, it appears to me, a higher standard of
environmental concern.

Against that, the fears induced when contemplating a
visit are depressingly familiar, and it will probably do little
to reassure the hesitant prospective tourist to say that the
chances of being injured in a road accident are much greater
than being involved in a terrorist incident in or near the

mountains – or anywhere else for that matter.

The *Mournes* are a small but highly varied and impressive granitic group. The eastern side has tor-topped steep-sided peaks, good ridges and long, deep valleys (routes 32 to 34, 40, 43), but the west is more plateau-like (routes 35, 41, 42). Unusually for an easily accessible area, there are few forestry plantations on the higher slopes. The Mournes rise to 850 metres/2,796 feet at bulky but unimpressive Slieve Donard (route 33). Much more memorable are Slieve Bearnagh (739 metres/2,396 feet) and Slieve Binnian (747 metres/2,449 feet) (routes 32, 34, 43). The good bus service facilitates rewarding end-to-end walks of the eastern Mournes in a not too strenuous day (route 34). Navigation on the higher peaks is greatly aided by the ubiquitous Mourne Wall which encloses the central Silent Valley and traverses all the main peaks, but care should be taken not to confuse it with other similar walls.

These mountains are much used by walking groups and this has strained the patience of farmers. Care should be therefore be taken to avoid trespass over farmland and to keep to the network of paths, which are well indicated on the maps, particularly the 1:25,000 map.

The *Cooleys* (route 36) are structurally part of the Mournes, though they lie across a narrow inlet in the Republic. A narrow rocky ridge with numerous small tops, they give good views but are not otherwise very interesting. Their indeterminate tops make navigation tricky, but in such a circumscribed area with some high-level roads, this is not a great difficulty.

The *Sperrins* (routes 37, 44) consist of gently swelling boggy moorland covering metamorphic schist and gneiss. The main range is broad and long (twenty-five kilometres/fifteen miles) but only one mountain wide, and rises to 678 metres/

2,240 feet at Sawel. The Sperrins can assuredly offer remote but definitely not over-exciting walking. Unfortunately, access problems at present (early 1994) make the area between Sawel and Dart out of bounds to walkers. The lower foothills, especially those on the south of the main range, are penetrated by long pleasant glens. South of the long Glenelly Valley, a lower section of the Sperrins runs parallel to the main range.

The *Antrim Plateau* (routes 38, 45) consists of moorland averaging only 300 metres/1,000 feet, some of which is of great ecological importance. Generally, it is less undulating than the Sperrins and cannot offer long "away from it all" walks. Slemish (437 metres/1,434 feet) is the most noteworthy of the several basaltic plugs (vertical columns of hard rock) which protrude from the moorland. The cliffs rimming the seaward side of the plateau are not high but are diversified by bizarre rock formations at their bases. These cliffs and the neighbouring moorland offer excellent views of nearby Scotland and of the glens and villages at their foot which are rightly renowned for their beauty.

Access to the mountains from the ferry ports of Larne and Belfast is easy. Newcastle, near the Mournes, is about ninety kilometres/fifty-five miles from Larne; the Antrim Plateau is very close and Maghera near the Sperrins is about sixty-five kilometres/forty miles away. The bus service radiates from Belfast and is quite comprehensive.

Roads and accommodation: roads within the mountain areas are good. Note in particular the B27, which runs through the Mournes and gives a good introduction by car to the range. There is plenty of accommodation available around the Mournes, where Newcastle is a large centre with lots of varied visitor accommodation, and on the coast below the Antrim

Plateau where Cushendun and Cushendall are two of several attractive villages. The three youth hostels along the Antrim coast mean that limited hostel-to-hostel walking along the plateau is possible. The Sperrins are not well provided with nearby accommodation, Plumbridge and Draperstown being the nearest towns and Strabane the best centre, though not all that close. The Cooleys have a good road system and several attractive villages offering accommodation. Of these, possibly the most scenic is Carlingford.

Local bus services: the Mournes and the Antrim Plateau are well served by Ulster Bus, with a route circumnavigating close to the higher Mournes (in July and August only) being particularly useful. In both these areas, buses facilitate A to B walks. The Sperrins are not so well served, especially the more attractive southern side. The Cooleys have a good service running along the coastal road.

Maps: with the exception of the southern part of the Cooleys, which has to make do with half-inch sheet 9, the maps of the whole region are excellent. All Northern Ireland is covered by maps in the 1:50,000 series (sheet 29 for the Mournes and much of the Cooleys, sheets 5 and 9 for the Antrim Plateau and sheet 13 for the bulk of the Sperrins). The Mournes also have a 1:25,000 map.

Route 32: N. High Mournes – Slieve Bearnagh

Map 29 (1:50,000) or "Mourne Country" (1:25,000).

Start at car park on left off B180 (J 312314). Take Ulster Way south for one kilometre, continue south-east to Hare's Gap (heading for prominent gate in wall ahead where paths diverge), follow Mourne Wall to climb Slieve Bearnagh

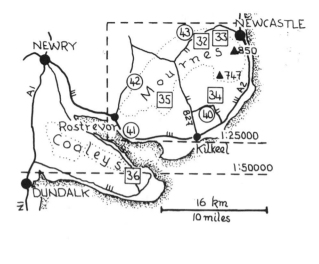

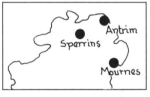

(large tors); when descending, keep clear of cliffs on right. Climb Slieve Meelmore (tower) keeping to right-most of two walls; climb Slieve Meelbeg. Leave wall to descend its north-west spur to Ulster Way and take Way to start.

> Distance: 11 kilometres.   Climb: 850 metres.
> Time: 3.75 hours.

Route 33: North High Mournes –
Slieve Donard

Map 29 (1:50,000) or "Mourne Country" (1:25,000).

Start at Tollymore car park (J 344326). Walk forest paths to forest edge at J 332312. Climb Luke's Mountain, Slievenaglogh, follow Mourne Wall east to Slieve Donard (tower, trig pillar) and south for one kilometre. Take Brandy Pad (path) north-west to Hare's Gap, climb Slievenaglogh following wall, retrace steps.

> Distance: 18 kilometres.   Climb: 1,150 metres.
> Time: 5.5 hours.

Route 34: South High Mournes –
Slieve Binnian

Map 29 (1:50,000) or "Mourne Country" (1:25,000).

Start at car park on north side of C313 (J 345219). Walk track north for 800 metres, then follow Mourne Wall to Slieve Binnian (large tors); walk to North Tor, Slievelamagan, col towards Cove Mountain, Cove Lough, path/track traversing Annalong Valley to start. There are several opportunities to vary the walk by heading east to the Annalong Valley, but beware of cliffs en route to this valley. The route can also be easily modified to finish in Newcastle.

> Distance: 14 kilometres.   Climb: 950 metres.
> Time: 4.5 hours.

Route 35: West Mournes

Map 29 (1:50,000) or "Mourne Country" (1:25,000).

Start at footbridge at J 264205 on Sally Brae Road, reached by turning right off C313, 0.7 miles south-west of Attical. Take path which starts just south of footbridge and runs west. Cross ford on river after 500 metres, then continue north-west, initially on path, to Eagle Mountain. Follow Mourne Wall to Pigeon Rock Mountain, take spur south, then descend south-west to track. To avoid private property near start, divert right, thus following stone wall.

Distance: 11 kilometres.   Climb: 750 metres.
Time: 3.5 hours.

Route 36: Cooleys

Map 29 (1:50,000).

Start in Carlingford (about J 1811). Take any road west out of the town, climb Slieve Foye (trig pillar), continue north-west along ridge to the Eagles Rock (point circa 520 metres), then west, passing lake at the White Bog (useful landmark) to point 457 metres and the Foxes Rock; descend west to Windy Gap. Walk north on road to reach waymarked Tain Trail. Take it past youth hostel and continue on it for 2.5 kilometres on coast and then on forest track/path running parallel to road.

Distance: 17 kilometres.   Climb: 750 metres.
Time: 4.75 hours.

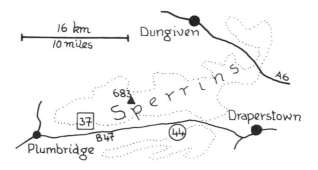

Route 37: Sperrins

Map 13 (1:50,000).

Start at road junction to north on B47 and just east of Henry's Bridge (H 516915). Take road/track along Glensass, turning right after approximately 2.5 kilometres to climb Mullaghclogher. From here follow fence along high ground east and north-east, climbing Mullaghasturrakeen, Mullaghclogha, Mullaghdoo. Continue east, north-east on high ground, then turn south onto track which crosses pass north-west of Dart. Walk south to B47, cross main valley and take road (partly Ulster Way) on its south side to Drumnaspar Bridge.

There are several opportunities to vary this route by taking any track running south, but beware access problems. Summits in this area are generally indistinct, so careful navigation is required in bad visibility.

> Distance: **25 kilometres.** Climb: **800 metres.**
> Time: **6.25 hours.**

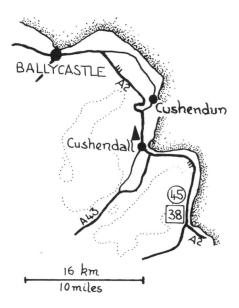

Route 38: Antrim Plateau

Map 9 (1:50,000).

Start at layby on A2, 2.0 miles north of Carnlough (D 295207).
Walk north 200 metres, take first left and first right onto
concrete road. Walk to farmhouse at end of road and take path
behind it to climb west through wood into open country.
Climb Turnly's Seat (rocky outcrop), Knockore (trig pillar) and
descend to west side of Lough Galboly. Follow cliffs clockwise

66

to just west of St MacNissi's College and descend on narrow path here to minor road parallel to A2. Take road to Loughan, fork right here onto minor road and take continuation track/A2 to start.

It is possible to extend the walk on the plateau towards the Trosks.

Distance: 13 kilometres.   Climb: 400 metres.
Time: 3.25 hours.

Route 39: Cuilcaghs

Map 26 (1:50,000).

Start at track running south, just south-west of entrance to Marble Arch (H 120336). Take track for 1.5 kilometres to demolished bridge, veer towards and then follow Sruh Croppa River to Tiltinbane. Watching for fissures in the ground, walk south-east to Cuilcagh (trig pillar). Descend east from summit to avoid worst of steep, grassy slope and pick up and follow Owenbrean River back to demolished bridge. Retrace steps to start. This area is described under the North Connaught region, but the route is given here because it is easier to access from Northern Ireland. Navigation is difficult on the extensive, featureless and wet moorland of most of this route.

Distance: 15 kilometres.   Climb: 600 metres.
Time: 4.5 hours (including 0.5 hours for wet terrain).

Easier Routes in Northern Ireland

Route 40

Map 29 (1:50,000).

Mournes: the Annalong Valley following the start of route 34.

Route 41

Map 29 (1:50,000).

Mournes: the forests east of Rostrevor starting at the Kilbroney car park at J 186180 just off the A2 and walking to Slievemartin. Highest point: 485 metres.

Route 42

Map 29 (1:50,000).

Mournes: Tievedockaragh starting at car park at J 224255 and following the east bank of Shanky's River for 3.5 kilometres to return via the summit. Highest point: 470 metres.

Route 43

Map 29 (1:50,000).

North Mournes: the start of route 32, then take the Brandy Pad, turning north into Newcastle. A long A to B walk, but on the path or track throughout. Highest point: 600 metres.

Route 44

Map 13 (1:50,000).

The low Sperrins south of Glenelly returning on the Ulster

Way. Start at Mount Hamilton (H 634942). Take road south, turn left onto side road after 300 metres and leave side road at convenient point to climb Corratary Hill. Walk south-west to Barnes Gap and return along road. Distance twenty-three kilometres, but car can be left at Barnes Gap to halve length. Highest point: 440 metres.

Route 45

Map 9 (1:50,000).

Antrim Plateau: as route 38, but return from the plateau by the same route.

Further Reading about Northern Ireland

North-East Irish Walks Guides, by Richard Rogers (Gill and Macmillan, reprinted 1991). Forty-seven detailed route descriptions.

Mourne Mountain Walks (Department of the Environment [NI], 1990). Ten route descriptions in plastic-card format.

Walking the Ulster Way, by Alan Warner (Appletree Press, new edition 1989). A journal and a guide.

North Ulster Walks, by James Hamill (Appletree Press, 1987). Twenty-two route descriptions, but only a few in mountain areas.

DONEGAL

. . . .

I ran, covered with perspiration and panting with heat,
to mount the topmost ridge [of Muckish]; and just as
we arrived there . . . and began to feast on the immense
vision of the earth and ocean beneath us, a vast murky
cloud from the Atlantic, big with sleet and moisture,
enveloped us as well as the whole top of the mountain
as with a night-cap, and made every thing so dark,
indistinct and dreary, that we could scarce see one
another.

Caesar Otway, *Sketches in Ireland,* 1827

. . . . .

The wildest and most spectacular mountains of this remote
region of fine rocky peaks interspersed with some of less
character are the North Donegal Highlands. These consist of
three parallel south-west to north-east lines of mountains, each
about fifteen kilometres/ten miles long, a layout which makes
looped walks a little difficult to plan.

Of the three ranges, that to the north (unnamed on the
maps), containing the striking quartzite scree-sided peak of
Errigal (751 metres/2,466 feet) and the flat-topped *Muckish*
(666 metres/2,197 feet) (routes 46 to 48, 60) is the most dramatic and spectacular. Errigal is the most symmetrical peak in
Ireland and boasts smallest summit; equally distinctive but
in stark contrast is the large cairn-studded plateau of Muckish.
These two peaks are connected by a fine range of hills cradling

high-level lakes. It is a pity, however, that in an area of few forestry plantations, a large one here blocks direct access from the south-east to this central section of the range.

The entire range forms the route of the east-west Glover Highlander, a marathon walk which takes place in September every year; a shortened version of this walk might be possible using the bus service which runs along the coastal road (N56). For this, the start of route 47 and the end of route 48 might be used.

The middle range, the granitic *Derryveagh Mountains,* rises to the great hump of Slieve Snaght (678 metres/2,240 feet) (route 49) south-west of the awesome Poisoned Glen. Backing the bare and sinister walls of this glen and extending into the area to its north-east and south-west, are long, straight, parallel lines of low cliffs running across the range. Though slow to negotiate, they add spice to an already rugged and scenic area.

The southern range, the *Glendowan Mountains,* is also granitic (for convenience, the name is applied to the whole line of mountains, not the smaller area designated on the Ordnance Survey maps). The lowest of the three, Glendowan's rolling wet moorland makes it of less interest than its northern neighbours. Most of the Glenveagh National Park (routes 50, 59) lies within the southern and middle ranges. The park, whose nucleus is a castle and a "chocolate box top" lake, contains a herd of red deer within a large area bounded by a deer fence. It can be crossed easily, but take care not to damage it.

North of the Highlands, some of the headlands facing the Atlantic, particularly Horn Head, give good cliff and coastal, rather than mountain, walks (routes 57, 58).

The *Inishowen Peninsula*, farther east, bears the imprint

of the south-west to north-east orientation of the Highlands. The hills here cover smaller areas and are lower, rising to 615 metres/2,019 feet at Slieve Snaght (Inishowen), which is unfortunately surrounded by extensive moorland (route 51). The tiny range of rocky serrated hills cut by the rugged Gap of Mamore (route 52) makes for far more diverse walking.

The other mountains of Donegal are to the south of the county and are separated from those farther north by bleak moorland which has only a few good distinct peaks (route 53). In the remote south-west the great bulge of wild land sometimes called *Rossaun*, to the north of Donegal Bay, yields a stupendous cliffscape at Slieve League (595 metres/1,972 feet) (route 54), which plunges from summit to ocean in mighty cliffs. There are some very remote cliff walks from Glencolumbkille north and east to Ardara (route 63) and some interesting country near the glacial valley of Glengesh (route 55). The remainder of the peninsula is not so interesting.

Farther east, north of Donegal town, are the *Blue Stacks* (routes 56, 62). They are guarded by exceptionally wet bogland whose waters augment the streams fed by foaming cascades from the several lakes of the interior. Luckily, the Donegal Way, which penetrates the range, is a handy means of access, though even it is usually quite soggy. The range itself is fairly small (about twenty kilometres/twelve miles long), with high points (they hardly qualify as peaks) which reach about 640 metres/2,100 feet. Signs of man (e.g. fences or walls) are notably absent. The range consists mainly of subdued granite country, sometimes in the form of huge pink granite slabs. This otherwise gently sloping terrain is broken by many low and some not so low cliffs. Because of its complicated terrain of irregular and unexpected cliffs and indeterminate peaks, good navigational skills are required, so the new 1:50,000 Discovery Series map is particularly welcome.

Access: the region is quite far from ferry ports and this difficulty is exacerbated by the generally bad state of Donegal's roads. Dublin is about 240 kilometres/150 miles from Letterkenny, and Larne is about 170 kilometres/105 miles away. There is an airport in Derry which is fairly close to the north-east of the region. There are no express bus services within North Donegal. A frequent express service runs between Donegal and Letterkenny and a once-a-week service runs west from Donegal town to Glenties in Rossaun.

Transport and accommodation in North Donegal: the N56 rounds the Highlands on three sides, linking a string of villages and small towns, any of which might act as a modest centre, though none is ideal for all areas. Creeslough, Dunfanaghy and Falcarragh are probably the best situated along the coast, and tiny Dunlewy the best inland. R-roads traverse parts of the valleys between the ranges but are circuitous and winding. The Lough Swilly Bus Company has an infrequent service along the coast which may be a help in devising A to B routes. Its present schedule, westward in the morning, particularly suits routes on the east of the Errigal – Muckish range. This company also serves Inishowen, where there are several seaside resorts to serve as small bases.

Transport and accommodation in South Donegal: there are only small villages in remote Rossaun – Glencolumkille is the best known; however, visitors will find at least modest accommodation everywhere. The roads on the peninsula are fairly poor, though access to the south of the Blue Stacks is quite good. Donegal, a comparatively large town, is the best centre for the Blue Stacks and indeed much of Rossaun. There are good local services west from Donegal town to Glencolumbkille and Glenties and an infrequent one beyond Glencolumbkille to Malinmore. There is also a good service through the Barnesmore Gap close to the Blue Stacks.

Maps: all of Donegal is covered by 1:50,000 maps, all but one in the Discovery Series. Note also the National Park one-inch map, which is just about satisfactory for the small area it covers. One advantage it has over other maps is that it shows cliffs explicitly. Another is that it comes free with the small entrance charge to the National Park. Watch that its flimsy paper doesn't disintegrate in rain.

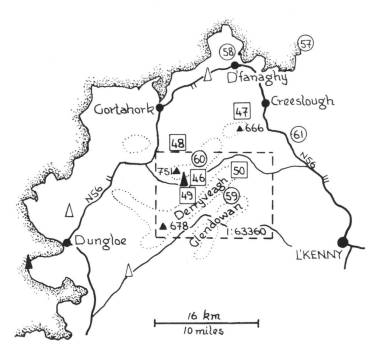

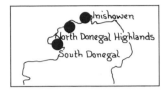

Route 46: North Donegal – Errigal

Map 1 (1:50,000), Discovery Series, or National Park map (one-inch).

Start on R251 at waymarked path west (B 940196), which begins 0.6 miles south-west of Altan Farm gates (named on pillar). This is one of several paths from R251, all of which merge. Take intermittent path in bogland, and later on east spur through scree slopes (here the path is clear and easily found) past Joey Glover memorial to nearby summit of Errigal (second summit is reached by short, narrow path). Retrace steps as far as prominent cairn, climb north-east to Mackoght. Walk to south-east corner of Altan Lough by descending east from Mackoght to avoid scree slopes both on its north side and south of the lough. Take track from south-east corner to R251. Walk can easily be extended to the Aghlas, route 48.

Distance: 10 kilometres.   Climb: 850 metres.
Time: 3.5 hours.

Route 47: North Donegal – Muckish

Map 2 (1:50,000), Discovery Series.

Start at the end of the tarmac on side road off N56

(C 005305), reached by turning south-west off N56 close to graveyard and driving 3.5 miles. Walk to end of track, climb to loading bays and then ascend steeply on path (important to avoid steep slopes) to quarry. Turn towards quarry face and take path on left of quarry to plateau. From trig pillar on east of Muckish plateau (not shown on map), descend east (some scrambling may be avoided by walking plateau a little clockwise). Walk north-east to Crockatee. Climb hill directly north of Lough Akeo, continue north to reach bog road leading to tarmac. Turn left for start. In bad weather this route is for the experienced only. An easy direct up-and-down route starts at the shrine at Muckish Gap, which is south of Muckish plateau. Note that there are several large cairns on the plateau, so that the trig pillar is a reassuring landmark.

Distance: 10 kilometres.   Climb: 650 metres.
Time: 3.5 hours (including 0.5 hours for
route-finding and steep descent).

Route 48: North Donegal – Aghlas

Map 1 and 6 (1:50,000), Discovery Series. RoI map 1 (half-inch) also satisfactory.

Start at fish farm gates near Procklis Lough (B 936255). To get there take road south from Falcarragh, fork left after 0.4 miles, right after further 0.7 miles, left after further 2.5 miles and continue for further 0.8 miles. Walk road north to cross bridge, take track immediately right to nearby farm. Walk south-east to Lough Nabrackbaddy, climb Aghla Beg (564 metres/1,860 feet), point 603 metres/1,900 feet, and continue clockwise on high ground to Aghla More, descending initially north-west to avoid steep slopes on north-east and south-west sides. Cross river on stepping stones at outlet from Altan Lough and walk track/road to start.

Distance: 10 kilometres.   Climb: 600 metres.
Time: 3 hours.

Route 49: North Donegal – Derryveaghs

Map 1 (1:50,000), Discovery Series, or National Park map (one-inch).

Start at prominent ruined church south of R251 at Dunlewy (B 929190). Walk south-east on track to nearby bridge, upstream on left (true) bank for one kilometre; climb Maumlack, descend south to Lough Beg, walk to Ballaghgeeha Gap (about B 955165), continue westwards to south of Poisoned Glen and south-westwards over high ground north-east of Slieve Snaght (escape possible northwards from high ground north-east of Slieve Snaght). Descend to Lough Slievesnaght (an easily identifiable landmark; other smaller lakes in this area are too similar to be useful); climb Slieve Snaght (large cairn). Descend steeply south-west to avoid cliffs to north, reaching Devlin River. Follow right bank to bridge crossed near start.

Route can be shortened by ascending easy gully in Poisoned Glen as start. To reach gully, follow main stream to right-angle bend near steep ground and then climb to obvious notch ahead to emerge close to Lough Atirrive Big.

> Distance: 15 kilometres.   Climb: 1,000 metres.
> Time: 5.5 hours (including 0.75 hours for
> negotiating low cliffs).

Route 50: North Donegal –
Glenveagh National Park

Map 6 (1:50,000), preliminary edition.

Start at the castle – the terminus of the shuttle bus from the visitor centre (which is at C 039232). Walk south-west along Lough Beagh, cross river on footbridge at south-west end of lake and ascend steeply with Astelleen Burn waterfall (not shown on map) on right. From valley behind waterfall, climb to col to south-east of Dooish, then Dooish. Climb point 555 metres, continue south-east to reach Lough Beagh at about C 002193 (take care near lakeshore on steep, slippery ground). Retrace steps to start. Deer culling may restrict access to this area in winter.

> Distance: 14 kilometres.   Climb: 550 metres.
> Time: 4.25 hours (including 0.5 hours
> for steep descent).

The shuttle bus does not run in winter. An alternative walk, then, is to start at the visitor centre, walk to the castle and take above route to Dooish. Take the ridge north-east over Saggartnadooish, point 391 metres to Misty Lough South. Walk spur east to small forest (not shown on map) near visitor centre, keeping to high ground on descent, as far as possible, to avoid wet areas.

Distance: 18 kilometres. Climb: 700 metres.
Time: 4.75 hours.

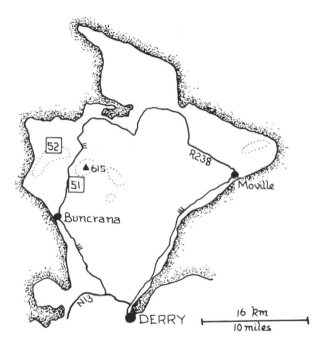

Route 51: Inishowen – Slieve Snaght

Map 3 (1:50,000), Discovery Series.

Start at Drumfree/Drumfries (C 384389). Walk road north-east,
taking nearby first track on right. At convenient point after

about one kilometre, leave it to climb Slieve Main (slow going through heather), Slieve Snaght, Slieve Snaghtbeg. Take spur north and then west (here heading towards prominent rocky Barnan More ahead) to reach track. Walk it to start.

Distance: 12 kilometres.   Climb: 600 metres.
Time: 3.5 hours.

Route 52: Inishowen

Maps 2 or 3 (1:50,000), Discovery Series. The latter is better for finding start.

Start near Butler's Bridge on minor road (C 359469). To get there drive south-west from phone kiosk in Clonmany for 0.2 miles; turn right and drive for further 0.7 miles. Follow intermittent path south-west initially on right (true) bank of stream through wooded Butler's Glen (slow going but escape possible to track on left); climb Raghtin More and Mamore Hill. Partly retrace steps, climb Slievekeeragh, take its north-east spur, coming left off it to meet track close to start. For a traverse of the entire ridge, a second car may be left at layby at C 294392.

Distance: 11 kilometres.   Climb: 750 metres.
Time: 3.5 hours.

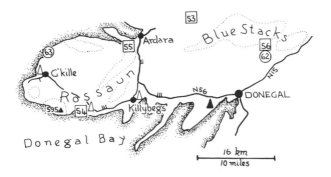

Route 53: Central Donegal

Map 11 (1:50,000), Discovery Series.

Start a few metres along track (B 890005). To get there take
R250 along length of Lough Finn, turn first left onto track.
Walk track east to first house. Turn right here to climb in or
near deep gully. Continue directly to Aghla Mountain (593
metres), whose trig pillar in area of numerous rocky hillocks
is especially useful. Keep to high ground past Castle Lough
to Knockrawer. Descend north to cross river and reach road
just south-west of road junction. Take road about 1.5 kilometres north-east to start.

Distance: 8 kilometres.   Climb: 500 metres.
Time: 2.5 hours.

Route 54: Slieve League

Map 10 (1:50,000), Discovery Series.

Start at Bunglass car park (G 558757), ignoring signpost "Slieve

League" at Teelin. Walk path along clifftop over Keeringear (mild scrambling avoidable by veering right) to reach east summit of Slieve League (cairn). Cross arete at One Man's Pass to reach main summit (trig pillar). Re-cross this arete to reach east summit and here descend east to oratory and wells. Take track and road to start.

> Distance: 12 kilometres.   Climb: 600 metres.
> Time: 4 hours (including 0.5 hours for
> scrambling and rough ground).

Route 55: Rossaun – Glengesh

Map 10 (1:50,000), Discovery Series.

Start at road junction (at G 716884) 0.7 miles south-west of Common Bridge. Walk side road south-east to farm, climb Common Mountain. Descend south-west spur and keep forest on left to cross road near top of pass, climb Croaghavehy, Glengesh Hill (indistinct top). Descend east, pick up driveway at two adjacent ruins to reach start (though exact route not critical).

> Distance: 11 kilometres.   Climb: 750 metres.
> Time: 3.5 hours.

Route 56: Blue Stacks

Map 11 (1:50,000), Discovery Series.

Start at end of tarmac on side road off road circling Lough

Eske (G 972870). (This side road is also route of Donegal Way, not shown on map.) Walk two kilometres north along Donegal Way to outlet stream from Lough Belshade; walk rough path to lake along right (true) bank, walk north-east side of lake, climb point 641 metres (note landmark of Lough Aduff directly to east). Continue along high ground to south-west, climbing point 642 metres and passing prominent quartz outcrop one kilometre to its south-west, to reach point 674 metres (trig pillar, shelter). Walk east, then south-east to Lough Gulladuff to avoid steep ground south of point 674 metres. Descend close to gorge near Lough Gulladuff to meet Donegal Way. Difficult navigation. See general description of Blue Stacks above to evaluate.

Distance: 12 kilometres.   Climb: 700 metres.
Time: 4.25 hours (including 0.75 hours
for difficult terrain).

Easier Routes in Donegal

Route 57

Map 2 (1:50,000) or map 1 (half-inch) hardly necessary.

North Donegal: a circuit of Melmore Head (starting near youth hostel at C 1243).

Route 58

Map 2 (1:50,000) or map 1 (half-inch) is useful but not essential.

North Donegal: from Hornhead Bridge area (C 0138), walk the cliffs along the east or west side of the promontory and return along the inland road. If taking west option, start on rough path just north of bridge. If taking east option, keep to beach for about 1.5 kilometres until past difficult vegetation inland.

Route 59

Map 6 (1:50,000) or National Park map (one-inch) useful but not essential.

The valley area of Glenveagh National Park following a there-and-back track south-west of the castle. The subsidiary valley betwen Farscollop and Kinnaveagh, which has a track/path, may also be explored.

Route 60

Map 1 (1:50,000) hardly necessary.

Errigal area: Altan Lough by following the track from Altan Farm gates nort-east of Dunlewy on R251 (B 952206). Highest point: about 350 metres.

Route 61

Map 1 (1:50,000) or map 1 (half-inch).

North Donegal: Loughsalt Mountain (about C 1226) starting at the car park north of Lough Salt, perhaps circumnavigating lake and returning along road on its west side. Highest point: 470 metres.

Route 62

Map 11 (1:50,000) or map 3 (half-inch).

South Donegal: the start of route 56 as far as Lough Belshade, returning by the same route. Highest point: 300 metres.

Route 63

Map 10 (1:50,000) or map 3 (half-inch).

South Donegal: starting about G 5285, walking the sea-cliffs north of Glencolumkille to Sturrall Head and onwards, and returning by same route.

Further Reading about Donegal

West and North: New Irish Walk Guides, by Tony Whilde and Patrick Simms (Gill and Macmillan, 1991). Twenty of the walks cover this region.

NORTH CONNAUGHT

It [Benbulbin] and its name are symbols of what is quite
one of the most picturesque as well as interesting areas
in Ireland; for it is a token – a kind of sign-board to
the cliff-walled valley-gashed limestone plateau that lies
behind it, and its name stands for the whole region.
Lloyd Praeger, *The Way That I Went*, 1937

. . . . .

This is a region of widely varying degrees of interest: small
blocks of mountains, some rimmed with rugged escarpments
but with few towering peaks, none of which exceed 650
metres/2,130 feet. They stretch from the Ox Mountains west
of Sligo town, higgledy-piggledy all the way east nearly to
Enniskillen in Northern Ireland, seventy kilometres/forty miles
away, covering a considerable part of South Ulster as well as
North Connaught.

The *Ox Mountains* (routes 64, 65) of west County Sligo
are unfrequented and it is easy to understand why. Gently
sloping, wet moorland rising reluctantly to 544 metres/
1,786 feet, the mountains are of little interest to anyone other
than the dedicated bog-trotter. Nevertheless, there are a few
areas, especially at the eastern end, which repay a visit. In
particular, an eastern extension, to the south-west and north-
east of Ballysadare (routes 65, 75), consists of low but rocky
well-shaped hills quite unlike the rest of the range.

Moving east, the hills roughly north of a line from Sligo

to Manorhamilton consist of a group of grassy limestone, and therefore dry plateaus, mostly surrounded by fearsome vertical escarpments riven here and there by great gullies. At the foot of the plateaus steep, grassy slopes predominate and the valleys between the plateaus often cradle narrow scenic lakes and curious, tiny, grassy hillocks. The highest point in the area is mast-topped Truskmore (647 metres/2,120 feet), though Benbulbin (526 metres/1,730 feet) under whose "bare head" Ireland's national poet, W.B. Yeats, is buried, is considerably better known, and Benwiskin (514 metres/1,702 feet), with its splendid profile best seen from near Ballaghnatrillick, is far more memorable (routes 66, 67, 72, 74).

The tiny *Castlegal range* (routes 68, 69, 71), unnamed on the maps, lies just to the north of Lough Gill and is an exception among these plateaus, since it has low but steep and rugged limestone hills, which make for slow progress. A small area on its southern flank, the *Doons*, consists of low, steep-sided hills with flat tops: a strange and highly individualistic landscape. This is a good area for days of low visibility. So is *Bricklieves/Carrowkeel* (route 73), a tiny area of plateaus topped by megalithic tombs and slashed by steep-sided trenches, which lies close to the N4 at Castlebaldwin.

These areas offer short but energetic scenic walks. At present considerably underrated, the new 1:50,000 maps should greatly increase their popularity.

Farther east again, roughly in a triangle bounded by Lough Allen, Manorhamilton and Enniskillen are other small blocks of hills (routes 39, 70). These are wetter and mostly duller than those to the west and not much frequented. Their generally gentle slopes are broken here and there by unexpected escarpments. The highest point is Cuilcagh (667 metres/

2,188 feet) on the international border. It is surrounded by formidable expanses of bogland. Route 39, covering Cuilcagh, is given under the Northern Ireland region because of better road access from the north.

Access: the region is quite far from cities and east-coast access points. Sligo is 240 kilometres/150 miles from Larne and 210 kilometres/130 miles from Dublin. The express bus system converges on Sligo, with the route to Enniskillen of some use in exploring the mountains. Sligo is also a railhead for mainline trains and a has a small airport.

Roads and accommodation: Sligo, a large town, is undoubtedly the best centre for the most attractive of these mountains, though Manorhamilton is also good. The roads which radiate from these towns (and others) give easy access, though directions must be carefully checked on unsignposted minor roads.

Local bus services traverse some minor roads near the mountains, especially the Castlegal Range, though they are generally infrequent. Particularly near Sligo town, these buses may be useful in organising A to B walks, though the bus timetable may have to be supplemented by a call to the local headquarters of Irish Bus in Sligo to find out the whereabouts of places not shown on the maps..

Maps: except for the western end of the Ox Mountains, the whole region is covered by maps at 1:50,000, the eastern part of the region by the Northern Ireland series (sheets 17 and 26), the western (and bulk) by the Republic's (sheets 16 and 25), the latter being only preliminary-edition maps but nonetheless of an excellent standard.

Route 64: Ox Mountains

Map 25 (1:50,000), preliminary edition – this map greatly exaggerates the extent and density of forest in the area.

Start at junction at north end of Ladies Brae Road (G 520301). Walk road south and at any convenient point leave it right to ascend steeply to Knockachree (indistinct summmit). Climb Knockalongy (trig pillar on plateau) over eroded peat giving slow going, and descend directly via sparse forest to Lough

Minnaun. Take firebreak at north-east end to forest track. Take track/road to start.

Distance: 11 kilometres.   Climb: 450 metres.
Time: 3 hours.

Route 65: Ox Mountains – Slieve Deane

Map 25 (1:50,000), preliminary edition – map shows more forest on south-east slopes of this part of range than in reality.

Start at car park south of Lough Gill (G 739314). Walk south along R287 for 500 metres, turning right here onto track. Continue to end as path and then take faint bridleway to meet track close to Lough Lumman. Walk past lough, still on track, and continue straight ahead on path where track swings left. Climb Slieve Dargan, Slieve Deane (trig pillar), point 266 metres. Drop to Lough Dagea and contour east to vegetated earth bank running from near point 208 metres, north-east to point 231 metres. At point 231 metres, head east to road (difficult vegetation), using forest track near corner of forest to reach it.

Distance: 6 kilometres.   Climb: 450 metres.
Time: 2.75 hours (including 0.75 hours for
difficult terrain).

Route 66: North Benbulbin Plateau

Map 16 (1:50,000), preliminary edition – see note below.
Start at Ballaghnatrillick (G 737502). Walk road (initially

south-east) for just over one kilometre, take driveway on right towards house at corner of forest, climb steps on house's left to reach firebreak. Walk firebreak to emerge at slopes of Benwiskin (forest here shown too high on map). Climb steeply to summit. Walk high ground anti-clockwise to head of Gleniff (escape possible here). Walk TV road to Truskmore (TV mast), climb Tievebaun following intermittent wall, descend west following right side of stream to reach road (when near road, veer away from stream to keep to easier ground).

Note: at present (early 1994) access difficulties make the above route out of bounds. The following route is an alternative until these difficulties are sorted out.

Distance: 17 kilometres.   Climb: 950 metres.
Time: 5 hours.

Route 66 (alternative): North Benulbin Plateau

Map 16 (1:50,000), preliminary edition.

Start near Glenade Lough (G 787486). To get there take R280 south through Largydonnell, pass church on left, take next right, turn left at T-junction, drive 0.1 miles and park here at laneway on right. Walk laneway to cross fence on left a few metres along, turn right and walk uphill to prominent Eagle's Rock (splendid rock formation; it is located 1.5 kilometres too far north-west on map). Enter pass between Rock and cliffs, and 600 metres beyond top of pass, at sheep pen, take path right to plateau. Keeping cliffs on right, walk to point nearly east of Tievebaun, climb to summit. Walk south to Truskmore

(TV mast) following intermittent wall. Walk east to plateau edge, then taking same path down to sheep pen. Continue east to meet track. On tarmac, turn left for start.

Distance: 13 kilometres.   Climb: 750 metres.
Time: 4.25 hours (including 0.25 hours for
boulders near Eagle's Rock).

Route 67: West Benbulbin Plateau

Map 16 (1:50,000), preliminary edition.

Start at gate beside guest house on north side of road (G 715424). To get there from Sligo, turn right onto minor road at church in Rathcormack. Fork right after 0.7 miles, turn right and drive a further 0.7 miles. Park considerately. Walk north initially on track, turn right and walk for about 800 metres to follow stone wall running parallel to and at foot of steep slope. Take grassy zigzag track below Pinnacle Gully (G 717436), leaving it to climb to gully entrance. Here take narrow passage left, climb to exit and contour clockwise to Benbulbin (no distinct top and trig pillar is set back from cliffs) and continue with cliffs on left. Descend King's Gully (at G 706440), here taking path/track on left of gully to near start.

Distance: 13 kilometres.   Climb: 500 metres.
Time: 3.5 hours.

Route 68: Castlegal Range

Map 16 (1:50,000), preliminary edition.

Start at junction on N16 (G 719411). To get there drive west along N16 and park at junction on right, 0.4 miles beyond sign "Glencar Lake 2k" on right (starting point needs care to find). Cross gate opposite junction to walk east across one field to track, initially indistinct. Turn right to take it, initially south, to edge of small plateau near point 331 metres. From here climb Cope's Mountain, skirt narrow grassy valley to north, climb point 452 metres, point 428 metres, descend south initially, then east to climb Crockauns, drop south-east to junction of walls and so reach road near point 374 metres. Return on side road. Two cars or bus facilitate a longer walk along the entire range ending east of Leean Mountain. In bad visibility, navigation is difficult because of numerous small summits.

Distance: 12 kilometres.   Climb: 600 metres.
Time: 4.25 hours (including 0.75 hours to
negotiate several low cliffs).

Route 69: Central Castlegal Range and the Doons

Map 16 or 25, both preliminary editions (1:50,000).

Start at junction on minor road (G 786369) reached from R286 by turning north just east of Parkes Castle, turning left at T-junction and taking first road right. Take road/track north, walking left from it at convenient point to climb point

407 metres and point 435 metres on Keelogyboy plateau (Sramore Lough is a useful landmark). Climb Sramore (point about 410 metres); keeping forest on left, climb Fawnlion. Climb Leean Mountain (trig pillar), descend south to track. Follow this to start.

Distance: 10 kilometres.   Climb: 650 metres.
Time: 4 hours (including 1 hour for difficult terrain).

Route 70: Dartry Plateau

Map 16 (1:50,000), preliminary edition.

Start at second adjacent bog track right (as one travels south) leading off minor road (G 858516). Follow bog track to end, walk north-west to plateau edge, climb Arroo (trig pillar), walk to Arroo Lough. Continue south, passing standing stone, to Lough Aganny, walk east one kilometre, then follow tributary of Glenaniff River northwards to bog track. Road to start.

Walk may easily be extended to west side of plateau overlooking R280.

Distance: 11 kilometres.   Climb: 400 metres.
Time: 3 hours.

Easier Routes in North Connaught

Route 71

The Doons starting in the same place as route 69. This is essentially a pottering area and a map is hardly necessary.

Route 72

Map 16 (1:50,000).

Glencar Waterfall, starting at the car park at Glencar Lough (G 760433). Take the track which crosses the stream behind the waterfall; then take concealed path on left to reach the plateau. Return by the Swiss Valley (about G 750441).

Route 73

Map 25 (1:50,000) hardly necessary, but if you have it note that Lough Availe, marked on this map, does not exist.

Bricklieves/Carrowkeel reached by leaving N4 at Castlebaldwin (G 5714) and following signs. This pottering area is described above. Give yourself plenty of time to negotiate low cliffs and bad vegetation.

Route 74

Map 16 (1:50,000).

Take the south side of the Benbulbin Plateau by ascending Pinnacle Gully and walking along the cliffs to King's Gully (variation of route 67). Spectacular gully scenery. Highest point: 430 metres.

Route 75

Map 25 (1:50,000).

Route 65 as far as Lough Lumman, returning by same route.

Further Reading about North Connaught

West and North: New Irish Walk Guides, by Tony Whilde and Patrick Simms (Gill and Macmillan, 1991). Eleven of the walks cover this region.

North Leitrim Glens, by David Herman (Shanksmare/NLGD Co, 1993). Detailed description of thirty-three varied routes in North Leitrim and Sligo.

MAYO

Standing on the edge of Croaghaun, it was difficult to believe that I was now on the edge of the highest sea cliffs in the British Isles, where the mountain suddenly comes to an end and falls 1,950 feet to the sea in a series of vast, rocky, partly grass-grown slopes. It was difficult to believe because beyond twenty feet in any direction, up, down, or sideways, it was impossible to see anything at all. All I could hear was the sea sighing far below, and the dismal crying of the gulls.

Eric Newby, *Round Ireland in Low Gear,* 1987

Mayo is a large county with several groups of mountains; unusually in Ireland, some of them take the form of small, isolated massifs. The hills are generally surrounded by large expanses of dreary bogs. Though there are massive and very remote sea-cliffs on the north coast (route 91), bounded inland by extremely dull mounds, the main mountain areas are around Clew Bay and in the very south of the county.

Let's work clockwise round Clew Bay starting with *Achill Island,* which is joined by a bridge to the mainland. One mountain here, Croaghaun (688 metres/2,192 feet) boasts as many as five corries, some tucked precariously into its tremendous northern sea-cliffs (routes 76, 87). The mountains themselves, grouped in a few small, discrete areas, are otherwise mundane. *Corraun,* a small peninsula close to

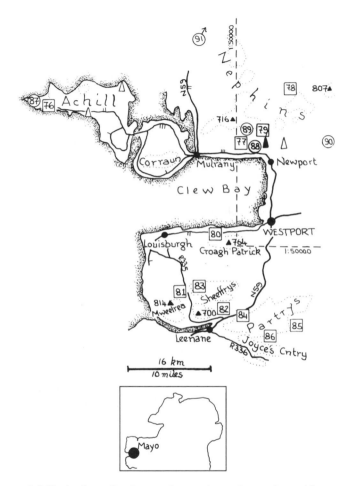

Achill, also has a few impressive corries on its northern side but is not otherwise over-exciting.

The *Nephins* (routes 77 to 79, 88, 89) are more formidable. They form a rough quartzite triangle rising for the most part

98

from blanket bog and monotonous forestry plantations which impede or bar access. The northern end of this range is undoubtedly the most remote in Ireland, with some areas being eight kilometres/five miles from an approach road (forestry roads come closer but may be barred to vehicles). This not very impressive distance indicates just how accessible all Irish mountains are; however, the time required to cover this distance is another matter. The Nephins are generally smoothly rounded, wet and bland but drop steeply in places into corrie lakes, especially at east-facing cliffs near its remote northern end. Corranabinnia (716 metres/2,343 feet) (route 77) is the climax of a good and comparatively accessible horseshoe from the south. Nephin itself (807 metres/2,646 feet), the highest peak, is a massive isolated mound far from the rest of the range and hardly worth climbing. A rough and very lonely path, the Bangor Trail, runs north for thirty kilometres/nineteen miles at low level through the Nephins, along their flanks and into dreary and wet moorland to their north.

Croagh Patrick (764 metres/2,510 feet) (route 80) dominates Clew Bay from the south as a ridge eight kilometres/five miles in length and provides excellent views of its sea-truncated drumlins. It has a fine, distinctive cone, but as a pilgrimage mountain the wide, ugly track leading to the summit and the ecclesiastical constructions on the summit do nothing to enhance it.

The mountains of *South Mayo* are generally more demanding than those farther north. The sandstone massif of Mweelrea (814 metres/2,688 feet) (route 81) lies directly north of the long, sinuous fiord of Killary Harbour. Commanding excellent views of ocean and mountain, it is a small but most attractive area, especially around the stern and forbidding gigantic corrie which truncates the north-eastern side of the massif. Unfortunately, this side is particularly badly depicted on the one available map (see below). Immediately to its east, the *Ben Gorm* group (700 metres/2,303 feet) (route 82) is another fine walking area, especially on its western side where it overlooks the sylvan pass at Delphi. The *Sheeffry Hills* (route 83), to the Ben Gorm group's north, are mostly flat uplands, though they have impressive corries on their northern flanks and a good east-west ridge walk at the western end.

The *Partrys* and *Joyce Country* comprising the triangle of hills east of the N59 and the R336 lie only partly in Mayo but are included here for convenience. The main feature is the Devilsmother (645 metres/2,131 feet) (route 84) at the western apex of the Partrys, which in spite of its threatening name offers lovely views along Killary Harbour. Of the rest of the Partrys, the corries that almost surround Maumtrasna (673 metres/2,207 feet), especially around Lough Nadirkmore (route 85) and the area north of Lough Nafooey, are rugged and scenic. However, the higher ground and the long north-east spur of this range are mostly wet, flat bogland. The part of Joyce Country directly to the north-east of the R336 (route 86) has nicely formed and, unusual for this area, grassy hills. Its south-west side falls in smooth slopes to the R336, with its spurs enclosing, in places, small secret valleys.

Access: Westport is about 260 kilometres/160 miles from Dublin, and Larne is about 340 kilometres/210 miles away. The region is not easily accessed and within the county even primary roads are not good. Knock Airport, in east Mayo, has regular flights to Dublin. A train service runs as far as Westport. A summer-only express bus service goes from Galway through Clifden and Leenane to Westport and another runs along the north side of Clew Bay. Other all-year express services run to Westport.

Roads and accommodation: the areas directly north and south of Clew Bay have few towns and not many villages; not unexpectedly, the road network is rather rudimentary. The minor roads running north from the Newport to Mulrany section of the N59 access the best of the area. Achill has much holiday accommodation but is not well situated for areas other than the island itself and perhaps Corraun. Newport and Mulrany are small towns close to the Nephins. There is a beautifully located youth hostel in these mountains. Westport is a good centre for the area around Clew Bay and not badly situated for South Mayo. Louisburgh is quite convenient to Croagh Patrick and much of South Mayo.

For South Mayo, Leenane (also spelt Leenaun), though tiny, is the best of the few centres and, as noted above, is served by express bus. It has the great advantage of being close to the mountains of Connemara, described in the next section. This area is not badly served by roads. The N59 passes close to the Partrys; the narrow R335 makes a scenic but tortuous route close to Mweelrea and the Sheeffrys and Ben Gorm to its east. The R336 passes along one edge of Joyce Country. There are few other motorable roads.

Local bus services follow the outline of Clew Bay, but not as one route. A private bus company operates a weekday bus service on the section of the N59 north of Mulrany. Leenane is served by local buses, but not the South Mayo mountains directly north of it.

Maps: most of this region is covered by maps 30, 37 and 38 in the Discovery Series. The major exception is the Nephins. The west of this range is covered on sheet 30 with the centre and east due to be covered in 1994. Sheet 37 is especially useful as it also covers a large swathe of Connemara. The half-inch sheets covering the area are sheets 6, 10 and 11, though if you have 10, 11 is hardly necessary. There are also uncontoured sketch maps in the "Bangor Trail Guide" (see Further Reading about Mayo below) and these show the Trail as well as an area of the Nephins not yet shown on the Discovery Series maps.

Route 76: Achill

Map 30 (1:50,000), Discovery Series.

Start at car park at Keem Bay (F 562045). Climb south to derelict building at point 198 metres. Walk north-west towards Achill Head turning back at developing knife-edge. Descend left to saddle, between sea-cliffs and Croaghaun, containing small lakes. Climb Croaghaun, descend north-east, following cliffs on left to top of cliffs south-east of Bunnafreva Lough West. Descend to Lough Corryntawy and Lough Acorrymore. Take direct route (pathless) or road to start.

> Distance: 11 kilometres.   Climb: 750 metres.
> Time: 3.5 hours.

Route 77: South Nephins

Map 6 (half-inch). Most of route is shown on map 30 (1:50,000), Discovery Series.

Start at Glendahurk Bridge (L 911979) by turning north off N59 about five miles west of Newport. Walk to Ben Gorm, then anti-clockwise on high ground to Corrannabinnia (point 2,343 feet, trig pillar) – steep ground to south and north-east of Corrannabinnia not adequately indicated on map. (Extension to Glenamong adds seven kilometres, climb 400 metres. Take care near cliffs on west of route.) Walk to point 1,437 feet, descend directly, picking up track towards start.

> Distance: 13 kilometres. Climb: 850 metres.
> Time: 4 hours.

Route 78: East Nephins

Map 6 (half-inch), but map 31 (1:50,000), Discovery Series, when available.

Start about one mile along minor road off R312 (about G 019087). Park considerately. Ford stream and climb spur south to Birreencorragh (trig pillar). Descend west, then take north-west spur to col south-east of point 920 feet. Walk down track/road to start.

> Distance: 10 kilometres. Climb: 550 metres.
> Time: 3 hours.

Route 79: Central Nephins

Map 6 (half-inch) – Bangor Trail Guide also useful; maps 30 and 31 (1:50,000), Discovery Series, when available.

Start at Treanlaur Youth Hostel (F 972013). Walk north on Bangor Trail to post 14, follow forest track upstream and cross bridge (footbridge at about F 967055, if in place, may also be used). Climb point 937 feet through scattered trees. Keep to high ground, avoiding some forestry, to climb 1,336 feet and Nephin Beg. Descend its south-west spur to Bangor Trail and follow it south-east, veering right off it to reach road on west side of Sramore River. Road to start.

Route 89 below may be used as an escape route.

Distance: 24 kilometres. Climb: 750 metres.
Time: 6 hours.

Route 80: Croagh Patrick

Maps 10 or 11 (half-inch). The boundaries of the Discovery Series maps fall awkwardly in this area, which is, anyway, an easy area in which to navigate.

Start at prominent car park at Murrisk (L 920824). Take pilgrim track to top of Croagh Patrick (ecclesiastical buildings), climb Ben Goram, descend towards Leckanvy reaching track on right bank of unnamed stream flowing north to Leckanvy. Keep on this bank to Leckanvy to avoid worst of high vegetation near village. Road to start.

Distance: 12 kilometres. Climb: 800 metres.
Time: 3.75 hours.

Route 81: Mweelrea

Map 37 (1:50,000), Discovery Series.

Start on R335 north of Doo Lough (L 829695). Walk south-west to cross stream near Doo Lough and ascend steep ground to right of corrie to reach summit plateau near Ben Bury (scrambling near top avoidable, from start only, by walking into corrie and taking path ascending left to right to reach plateau at lowest point of corrie rim). Walk to Mweelrea, retrace steps to edge of corrie and walk east with cliffs on left. Keep steep ground on left to continue downwards, avoiding subsidiary spur diverging right, to ford stream at ruin at L 846666. Walk road to start.

There is an easier approach to Mweelrea from Delphi Adventure Centre, just south of Fin Lough.

Distance: 16 kilometres.   Climb: 1,050 metres.
Time: 6.5 hours (including 1 hour for scrambling and steep descent).

Route 82: Ben Gorm

Map 37 (1:50,000), Discovery Series.

Start at car park near Ashleagh Falls (L 894645). Take track upstream a short distance, then walk spur west to Ben Gorm, Ben Creggan (693 metres). Descend spur east for two kilometres, walk directly to start crossing two streams (very wet ground, so there and back to Ben Creggan is advisable after wet weather).

Distance: 11 kilometres.   Climb: 800 metres.
Time: 3.5 hours.

Route 83: Sheeffry Hills

Map 37 (1:50,000), Discovery Series.

Start at car park on R335 (L 844677). Climb north to point 772 metres. Continue east on narrow ridge to point 762 metres (trig pillar). Walk one kilometre east to two small lakes, then descend south-east spur, keeping forestry on right to meet side road. Walk 5 kilometres on road to start. Walk can be extended to point 742 metres, descending on south-east spur, keeping forest on right.

Distance: 12 kilometres.   Climb: 800 metres.
Time: 4 hours.

Route 84: Devilsmother

Maps 37 and 38 (1:50,000), Discovery Series; maps 10 or 11 (half-inch) may suffice.

Start around Glennacally Bridge on N59 (L 936657). Choose convenient point to climb Devilsmother (twin summits) on north spur. Descend north-east, east to col, climb point 617 metres/2,039 feet and contour anti-clockwise past Maumtrasna to descend steep ground on west-running spur (Luga Kippen) to road.

Distance: 15 kilometres.   Climb: 950 metres.
Time: 4 hours.

Route 85: Partrys

Map 38 (1:50,000), Discovery Series.

Start at end of road within one kilometre of Dirkbeg Lough (M 003657). To get there take road towards Toormakeady from road along north side of Lough Nafooey, turn left at sign "Killateeaun", cross bridge over Owenbrin River, turn next left (just before post office) and fork left shortly onto track. Climb spur to north of Dirkbeg Lough and continue anti-clockwise round corries of this lake and Lough Nadirkmore. Walk east to points 584 metres and 514 metres, descend north-east to cross road that ends at Lough Nadirkmore and continue to track leading to Dirkbeg Lough.

> Distance: 11 kilometres. Climb: 520 metres.
> Time: 3.5 hours.

Route 86: Bunnacunneen

Map 38 (1:50,000), Discovery Series.

Start at junction of minor road and track 0.3 miles north of R336 (L 926570). Walk track east upstream and continue to stream's source forking right at major junction after 700 metres from start to reach col near point 335 metres. (Alternatively: walk spur to south of this stream.) Walk north to Bunnacunneen (extension south-west to Lugnabrick adds six kilometres, climb 150 metres). Descend directly west to road.

> Distance: 11 kilometres. Climb: 520 metres.
> Time: 3.5 hours.

Easier Routes in Mayo

Route 87

Map not necessary.

Achill Head (start of route 76 but return from small lakes on saddle col facing Croaghaun). Beware cliffs, especially in high winds.

Route 88

Map not necessary but Bangor Trail guide useful.

Circuit around Treanlaur Youth Hostel using Bangor Trail and road along Lough Feeagh.

Route 89

Map 6 (half-inch) but Bangor Trail guide more useful.

Nephins: start and end of route 79, walking by track and firebreak to unnamed lake at F 944074 to make shorter circuit. Highest point: 280 metres.

Route 90

Map 6 (half-inch).

Croaghmoyle (about M 1098). From R312 near Beltra Lough climb Birreen and continue north to Croaghmoyle. Descend directly to road. Highest point: 420 metres.

Route 91

Map 6 (half-inch).

North Mayo sea-cliffs. Take road east at junction just south of Porturlin (F 883418). Walk to cliffs and continue along them indefinitely, returning by same route.

Further Reading about Mayo

West and North: New Irish Walk Guides, by Tony Whilde and Patrick Simms (Gill and Macmillan, 1991). Fifteen of the walks cover this region.

   County Mayo – The Bangor Trail Guide, by Joe McDermott and Robert Chapman (Mayo Co. Council, 1992).

   West of Ireland Walks, by Kevin Corcoran (O'Brien Press, 1993). Seven of the walks cover this region. The emphasis is on flora and fauna.

CONNEMARA AND THE BURREN

. . . .

Some of our party (on Ben Lettery) called for the provision basket. It was little short of treason against the majesty of nature, to fix those eyes on rolls and cold beef, which ought to have been directed to one of the noblest views of Cunnemarra.

Caesar Otway, *Sketches in Ireland,* 1827

. . . . .

First *Connemara,* that is the Twelve Bens, the Maamturks and the Benchoonas. All three ranges are in west Galway and separated from the mountains of south Mayo only by Killary Harbour. This is a small but highly varied area, much of it bereft of the evidence of humankind, yet not all that remote, and in all very rewarding. The Burren in County Clare is quite far away from Connemara and is included in this region only because it fits in even more incongruously elsewhere than it does here.

The *Twelve Bens* (routes 92 to 94, 104), also incorrectly called "the Twelve Pins", a magnificent cluster of steep-sided, bare, rocky quartzite "haystacks", cover a tiny area (less than ten kilometres/six miles in any direction). Some of the Bens are in the Connemara National Park and contain the nucleus of a recently introduced herd of red deer.

Though they rise to only 730 metres/2,395 feet at Binn Bhan/Ben Baun (route 93), the seventeen or so peaks in this range appear to be very much higher and the long, steep descents and re-ascents between peaks make most walks within them quite arduous. Navigational problems are not as acute as might appear at first glance – the narrow ridges virtually exclude all but the most gross errors, though these, if they occur, could involve lengthy and difficult retreats. Because of the lack of vegetation on the tops and slopes, these hills are exceptionally dry underfoot. In contrast, the valleys are normally very wet and should be avoided. The most popular routes are high-level circuits of the tight horseshoes surrounding the valleys (routes 92 to 94).

Like the Twelve Bens, the *Maamturks* (routes 95 to 97), are a bare, rocky quartzite range rising to a somewhat lower height, Binn idir an Da Log (703 metres/2,307 feet) (route 95) being the highest peak. Like the Bens, they are generally dry underfoot and command marvellous views. Here the resemblance ends because, as has been observed: "The Maamturks are the Bens, straightened out and with the tops sheared off". The Maamturks form two shallow arcs (the smaller is named on the maps as part of Joyce Country), in all about twenty kilometres/twelve miles long. It is this near-linear configuration which makes looped walks difficult to devise. The tops form a virtual plateau slashed by a set of steep-sided passes which are heart-breakingly arduous to traverse on routes along the spine of the range. This plateau and the numerous unwanted cairns in places make navigation particularly difficult in poor visibility, so that the excellent mapping is of a great help. Careful study on the map of the details of the proposed route is advisable.

The Western Way runs through a gap in the Maamturks and along its flanks; though it is not waymarked at present, it is useful in forming the lowland section of looped walks. The

Maamturks Walk, considered by many to be the toughest of Ireland's marathon walks, takes place every year in May or June; the route is usually north-west to Leenane.

The *Benchoonas* (routes 98, 99, 101) are the hills between Killary Harbour and the N59. A small area of modest hills rising no higher than 601 metres/1,973 feet at Garraun, they nonetheless provide great geological interest and command lovely views. For days of low cloud there is an easy and scenic walk along the south shore of Killary Harbour south-east of the youth hostel (route 101).

Though not really a highland area – the hills reach only 346 metres/1,134 feet – the strange lunar-like karstic landscape of the *Burren* (routes 100, 105) of north-west Clare is certainly worth a visit. From a distance, each hill looks like a stack of grey discs, each smaller than the one directly below it. Closer to, the limestone pavements across which one walks (beware of the numerous grooves in the rock) are short, crumbly, easily climbed cliffs. It is particularly rewarding to walk the Burren in May, when the numerous varieties of plants which thrive here are in bloom. The waymarked Burren Way takes in much of the area. There is a comparatively easy marathon walk in the Burren in August.

Access: the N6 (Dublin to Galway road), the usual approach to Connemara, is fairly good, though the roads west of Galway are narrow and bumpy. Clifden, on the remote western outskirts of the region, is about 300 kilometres/185 miles from Dublin; Larne is about 400 kilometres/250 miles and Rosslare Harbour about 350 kilometres/215 miles away. Galway has the nearest railway station and a small airport. There are express buses to Clifden from Galway via Roundstone and from Westport via Leenane, both operating in the summer only.

Roads and accommodation: travel by road within Connemara is surprisingly easy. The N59 runs near all the ranges and the R344 runs between the Maamturks and the Twelve Bens but is of little use for the latter because a line of lakes and a swathe of forest greatly impede an approach from the road. The biggest centre by far in Connemara is Clifden, though even it is modest. There are several other smaller centres, for instance Letterfrack and Recess. Tiny Leenane, as stated previously, is well placed for much of Connemara and equally well placed for the mountains of South Mayo.

Local bus services follow variations of the express routes (they leave the N59 to call to surrounding villages) so that the region is generally quite well served by public transport. *The Burren* is quite easy to access, has several small towns close to it and has express bus services running through Ballyvaughan and Lisdoonvarna. The local bus service is quite poor.

Maps: all except the very south of the region is covered by sheet 37 of the Discovery Series (which also covers the best of the Mayo region), with a small area of the Maamturks covered by sheet 38. Unfortunately, the sheet boundaries do not aid walkers, so that the southern parts of the Bens and Maamturks are excluded, and there is an awkward border through the Maamturks.

Though it may now be a little out of date, the Connemara map/guide contains a map at 1:50,000 which is explicitly designed for walkers. Its boundaries neatly encompass the three ranges in Connemara and it shows cliffs comprehensively, the only map in the Republic to do so. For this reason, it is given as the reference map for the area it covers.

Note that most mountain names are in Irish on this map and therefore unfamiliar to most walkers and indeed probably to locals (though it has to be said that locals probably find the English version unfamiliar!). Unfortunately, the paper used is flimsy and it would be worth while reinforcing it if it has to take more than minimal use. The Burren is covered by the usual

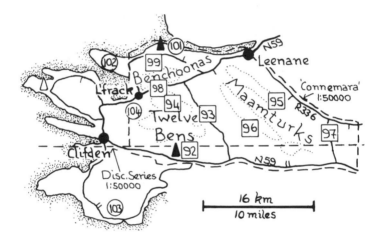

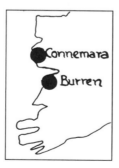

half-inch map (sheet 14), but look out for T.D. Robinson's stylish map of the Burren on a scale of 1:35,200. It is uncontoured; escarpments and small-scale features are, however, shown and these make it quite adequate for walkers.

Route 92: South Twelve Bens – Gleann Chochan Horseshoe

Connemara map (1:50,000).

Start at Ben Lettery Youth Hostel on N59 (L 777483). Climb Ben Lettery/Binn Leitri directly from youth hostel; climb Binn Gabhar. Climb Binn Bhraoin by easily avoidable scree slope, walk along summit plateau north, then north-east and take steep rocky descent north-east (not east) to col at Mam Eidhneach (L 788527) (escape possible here but make for track at L 806501 to minimise wet ground). Climb Bencollaghduff, descend to col at Mam na bhFonsai, climb east, then south-east to Binn Chorr. Climb Derryclare and, to avoid cliffs to right, continue south for 1.5 kilometres before veering right to pick up track. If, alas, there is no transport here, walk track for two kilometres and N59 for 1.5 kilometres.

Distance: 16 kilometres.   Climb: 1,600 metres.
Time: 7.5 hours (including 1.5 hours for
steep descents).

Connemara map (1:50,000).

A short introductory walk in the Bens is to take the above route to Binn Gabhar, retrace steps to cairn between it and Ben Lettery and climb Binn Ghleann Uisce. Descend west to forest

115

(shown much higher on map than in reality) and follow it to track. Track and N59 to start.

Distance: 10 kilometres.   Climb: 700 metres.
Time: 3.25 hours.

Route 93: North-East Twelve Bens – Gleann Eidhneach Horseshoe

Connemara map (1:50,000), or map 37 (1:50,000), Discovery Series.

Start at junction of side road and R344 (L 819562). Walk side road for 200 metres, then climb Knockpasheemore, Binn Bhan (trig pillar), descend steeply (avoiding crags) to Mam Eidhneach (escape possible here). Climb Bencollaghduff, descend to col at Mam na bhFonsai, climb north-east to Binn an tSaighdiura, Binn an Choire Bhig, descend steeply (avoiding crags) to river at about L 812551, cross it here and meet track.

Distance: 13 kilometres.   Climb: 1,200 metres.
Time: 5.75 hours (including 1.25 hours for
steep descents).

Route 94: North Twelve Bens

Connemara map (1:50,000), or map 37 (1:50,000), Discovery Series.

Start at end of tarmac on minor road (L 796574). Take track initially south and at its end climb Binn Fhraoigh (detour to

Binn Bhan adds two kilometres, climb 200 metres), Meacanach. Walk north to climb Binn Bhreac, Maolan. Descend north-west spur to unnamed section of lake between Kylemore Lough and Poll an Chapaill and take path/track to start.

Distance: 13 kilometres.   Climb: 1,050 metres.
Time: 5.5 hours (including one hour for
steep descents).

Route 95: Maamturks – Failmore/Gleann Fhada Horseshoe

Connemara map (1:50,000), or maps 37 and 38 (1:50,000), Discovery Series.

Start at layby on minor road (L 932528). Walk south-west along Western Way for about 1.5 kilometres; here climb directly west to Binn Mhairg, Binn Chaonaigh, Binn idir an Da Log (on this leg note zigzag route to keep to high ground). Descend to near Lough Mham Ochoige avoiding crags, walk north-east to point 438 metres, take ridge east to Cnoc na gCorr, descending south to road to avoid crags.

Distance: 16 kilometres.   Climb: 1,050 metres.
Time: 5.5 hours (including 0.5 hours for
steep descent).

Route 96: Central Maamturks

Connemara map (1:50,000), or map 37 (1:50,000), Discovery Series.

Start at car park on R344 (L 847533). Walk road east, south-east for about two kilometres, ascend north-east here (at about L 866526) into high valley. Climb to Mam Ochoige, climb Cnoc na hUilleann (initial cairn visible on this ascent marks edge of plateau). Walk north, north-west to Binn Bhriocain. Walk north-east for 800 metres, then descend initially north-west to pass at Mam Tuirc and west to Western Way. Turn left onto Way (it may not be evident at first; simply keep to foot of slope on left). Take it to road following electricity poles towards end if Way unclear. Road to start. Difficult navigation on tops in bad visibility.

Distance: 16 kilometres.   Climb: 800 metres.
Time: 5 hours (including 0.5 hours for
steep descent).

Route 97: East Maamturks

Connemara map (1:50,000).

Start at junction 0.3 miles south-west of Maam Bridge/An Mam (L 963523). Walk road south for about 2.5 kilometres to near top of pass, climb initially south-west to Corcog, Mullach Glas (remains of fence useful for navigation on these two climbs), Binn Mhor (trig pillar), Binn Ramhar. Descend to Mam Ean. Turn right to walk Western Way to start.

Distance: 18 kilometres.   Climb: 1,100 metres.
Time: 5.75 hours (including 0.25 hours
for steep descent).

Route 98: South Benchoonas

Connemara map (1:50,000), or map 37 (1:50,000), Discovery Series.

Start at Kylemore Abbey car park (L 748585). Ascend south on path to statue (signposted from abbey, this path is essential to find to avoid rhododendrons). Climb Duchruach (indistinct summit), descend to Lough na Crapai veering left to avoid steep ground, climb steeply to Altnagaighera (no distinct summit; instead conglomerate rock outcrops along spur). Climb Garraun, take spur south and continue close to stream, veering slightly right from it near N59 to avoid farmhouse left and rhododendrons right. Turn right onto N59, take gated track right after one kilometre and pass abbey.

> Distance: 9 kilometres.   Climb: 900 metres.
> Time: 3.5 hours.

Route 99: North Benchoonas

Connemara map (1:50,000), or map 37 (1:50,000), Discovery Series.

Start on road at north-west end of Lough Fee (L 780621). Cross bridge and take track/path along south-west side of Lough Fee for about 1.5 kilometres. Climb to point 283 metres, Garraun, Binn Chuanna. Descend north-west to avoid steep ground, cross stepping stones at L 769633 to reach road.

> Distance: 8 kilometres.   Climb: 600 metres.
> Time: 2.75 hours.

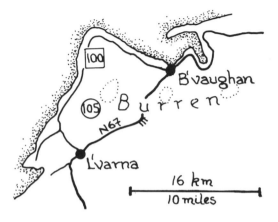

Route 100: The Burren

Map 14 (half-inch) or the Burren map (1:35,200).

Start at junction of minor road on R477 (M 144088). Walk north along R477, turn first right onto track, walk 400 metres, then continue straight ahead onto indistinct path where track swings right. Walk path/track towards Black Head, then climb point 1,045 feet, Gleninagh Mountain (trig pillar), descend to path to east (escape route north-east from here to R477). Turn right onto this path, veering right where path is indistinct, to reach road at Feenagh. Take roads to start.

> Distance: 15 kilometres.   Climb: 450 metres.
> Time: 4.25 hours (including 0.5 hours for low cliffs).

Easier Routes in Connemara and the Burren

Route 101

Connemara map (1:50,000), or map 37 (1:50,000), Discovery Series.

Killary Harbour: start at youth hostel (L 769651) and walk south-east along path close to fiord. On return pick up track which diverges inland (close to coastal path, it is indistinct), and further on has escarpment on right, to reach road south-east of youth hostel.

Route 102

Map 37 (1:50,000), Discovery Series, or map 10 (half-inch).

Tully Mountain (about L 6762): climb from north-east and walk along summit ridge. Return can be made along shore. Highest point: 360 metres.

Route 103

Map 10 (half-inch) hardly needed.

Errisbeg (about L 6940): climb from west. Exceptional views for little effort. Highest point: 300 metres.

Route 104

National Park map (one-inch) sufficient.

Diamond Hill (about L 7357): climb from the National Park centre to its west, but note that erosion in this area may make it out of bounds. Highest point: 450 metres.

Route 105

Burren map by T.D. Robinson

The Burren: all this area is low level and good for pottering about. Apart from the area mentioned in route 100 above, the areas centred on Turlough (about M 2805) and Mullaghmore (about R 3396) from the north are good examples of the area's terrain, though there may be access difficulties around Mullaghmore at the time of writing (early 1994).

Further Reading about Connemara and the Burren

West and North: New Irish Walk Guides, by Tony Whilde and Patrick Simms (Gill and Macmillan, 1991). Eighteen of the walks cover this region.

The Mountains of Connemara, by Joss Lynam, Justin May and T.D. Robinson (1988). Eighteen route descriptions and an excellent 1:50,000 map.

West of Ireland Walks, by Kevin Corcoran (O'Brien Press, 1993). Seven of the walks cover this region. The emphasis is on flora and fauna.

KERRY

. . . .

. . . it was odd how, standing in mist among
ecclesiastical-looking cairns [on Brandon], we looked
down and saw that Smerwick and Ballyferriter were
enjoying a day of sunshine, Brandon Head was rainy,
and Mount Eagle was in cloud. Climbing west of Dingle
is deceptive, a succession of false summits, each windier
than the last; but from the heights of Brandon the whole
peninsula is spread out like a topographical map, path
and road, cove and headland.

> Paul Theroux, *Sunrise with Seamonsters,* 1985

. . . . .

The mountains of Kerry (and those of West Cork which are
included here) are a large and complex tangle of predominantly
old red sandstone rock. To make some sense of them, the
region is considered here in three sub-regions, Dingle, Iveragh
and Beara, corresponding to the three main peninsulas and
their mountainous hinterlands. Each of these three, where
necessary, is further broken down into individual ranges.

The only general comments that might usefully be made
about Kerry are that it contains most of the highest mountains
in Ireland, including all but two of the Munros; that the whole
region is remote and because of the long, jagged peninsulas
difficult to access; that the sea or its inlets are never far away;
that good centres are easier to find in the east than in the
remote west; and lastly, and perhaps most importantly, that

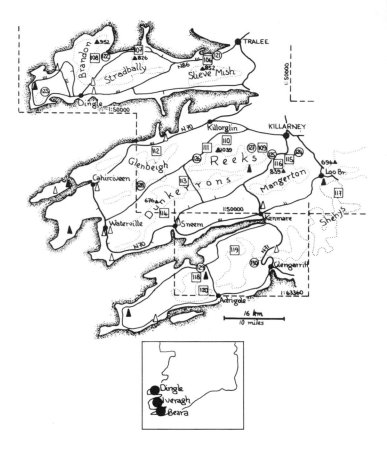

the whole region is so attractive that you are unlikely to regret the effort of getting there!

The *Dingle Peninsula,* the northmost of the Kerry peninsulas, is divided by the two roads which cross it diagonally into three mountain groups, which are more scenic and wilder as one progresses westward. The Slieve Mish range in the east rises to 852 metres/2,796 feet at Baurtregaum (routes 106, 121). These hills are very dull and bland on their southern slopes, but the northern side facing Tralee Bay is much sharper and more inviting. Immediately west is the Stradbally group (route 107), a range of fine peaks. Its northern edge, where Beenoskee rises to 826 metres/2,713 feet, is especially attractive. Its southern aspect is much duller, degenerating to bogland in places. The Brandon group to its west takes many of the walkers who would otherwise visit this area.

The *Brandon* group, of which Brandon itself (routes 108, 122) is the most notable and highest at 952 metres/3,127 feet, is undoubtedly the main attraction of the peninsula. Facing north-west in stern cliffs to the ocean and dominating the western skyline in jagged outline, this massif (especially its eastern and northern sides) is most striking. Routes from the east, which take in a string of paternoster lakes in rugged corries, are exceptionally scenic. Incidentally, this far western end of the peninsula (route 123) is exceptionally rich in archaeological remains and is one of the few remaining strongholds of the Irish language.

The *Iveragh Peninsula* has the highest mountains in Ireland; while not everyone would say that they are the most scenic mountains, few would dispute their attractions for the hill walker. Their layout is quite complex and the four sub-ranges detailed here are more for descriptive purposes than for geographic exactitude.

The general trend is north-east to south-west following the lines of the drowned valleys which bound the peninsula. The Macgillycuddy's Reeks (usually called simply the "Reeks") lie directly west of Killarney. Westward is the horseshoe of hills at Glenbeigh, including the Knocknadobar range. South of the

Reeks and stretching to the south-west corner of the peninsula run the Dunkerrons (name probably not authentic) and paralleling it, but farther east, the Mangerton range.

To look at these ranges in more detail, let's start again at the *Reeks*. At the eastern end, the heather-covered Purple Mountain group (route 109) may be considered part of the Reeks but is a trifle mundane. West of the great slash of the Gap of Dunloe (route 127) are the Reeks proper: a long line of hills (the latest Ordnance Survey maps count six tops over 914 metres/3,000 feet) which fall away spectacularly in great cliffs to the north (routes 110, 126). At the western end is the semi-circle of hills around the corrie of Coomloughra which contains the three highest peaks in Ireland: Caher (1,001 metres/3,200 feet), Carrauntoohil (1,039 metres/3,414 feet) and Beenkeragh (1,010 metres/3,314 feet), the latter two connected by a striking knife-edge, the Beenkeragh ridge (route 111). It hardly needs mentioning that a circuit encompassing these three peaks gives a memorable and exciting day.

Glenbeigh (route 112) consists of rather dull moorland broken on its north-east side by a set of magnificent lake-filled corries separated by narrow spurs. The small Knocknadobar range directly to its west has good views of its own and neighbouring peninsulas, but it otherwise comparatively mundane.

The *Dunkerrons* run from Broaghnabinnia (745 metres/2,440 feet) south-west along the spine of the peninsula for about forty kilometres/twenty-five miles. Mullaghanattin (773 metres/2,539 feet) (route 113) is the highest peak, and a circuit from north or south makes a magnificent walk. From the north, walkers will take in the complex tangle of bare and convoluted hills around Cloon Lough. South-westwards from Mullaghanattin the spine continues over Knocknagantee (676 metres/

2,220 feet) and Coomcallee to dwindle into lower hills to its
west and south-west (routes 114, 128). This whole area south-
west of Mullaghanattin is a remote and rugged one, much of
it offering fine views of the sea and off-shore islands. In places,
progress is greatly impeded by sandstone slabs similar to those
described below under Beara. Walking in the area roughly
south and west of Knocknagantee is hampered by poor
mapping (see below).

The *Mangerton* range runs south-westwards from the
gently sloped mounds of the Paps (696 metres/2,284 feet),
through a low but varied area south of Lough Guitane (routes
115, 124), an excellent area for days of low visibility. It
continues over the plateau of Mangerton (839 metres/2,756
feet) (route 116), whose chief glory are its huge north-facing
corries, and terminates south-west in duller country directly
east of the N71.

Lastly, in Iveragh, I should mention Killarney National Park
and the Kerry Way. The National Park is over one hundred
square kilometres/forty square miles in extent and includes
much of the Reeks as well as a large area south of Killarney.
Its attractions include a herd of magnificent red deer, the only
true native red deer species in Ireland. They may be seen on
the slopes of Mangerton and Torc. The park also contains the
most extensive area of natural woodland in the country. The
Kerry Way traverses much of the peninsula starting in Killarney
and completes a loop parallel to and at a higher level than the
main road round the peninsula. It also has spurs from some
of the villages on the peninsula. Much of it runs through
exceptionally scenic country and can be walked using hostel
accommodation.

The *Beara Peninsula* is the southernmost of the three main

Kerry peninsulas; along with it, I will include the Shehy Mountains of West Cork (route 117). High ground reaching 700 metres/2,300 feet runs from the Shehys westward to the tip of the peninsula fifty-five kilometres/thirty-five miles away. Memorable circuits can be made around the hills surrounding the several valleys on the north of the peninsula (routes 118 to 120, 129). To the east, the high ground at the spine of the range sometimes degenerates into moorland, though the views are not impaired. Much of the uplands is composed of long corrugations of steeply angled sandstone slabs which can greatly impede walking "across the grain", while lower down the high, luxuriant vegetation which flourishes in the mild and humid climate can achieve the same effect. A long-distance walk circumnavigates the peninsula.

Access to the Kerry Region: the region is quite distant from cities and east coast ports. Killarney, on the eastern margins of the region, is 300 kilometres/190 miles from Dublin and 270 kilometres/170 miles from Rosslare Harbour. There are rail connections to Tralee and Killarney and an airport about midway between these towns. The express bus routes travel through the towns to the east of the peninsulas, though they do not run onto them.

Facilities and mapping in the Dingle Peninsula: the peninsula is moderately well traversed by the N86 and R560, though Brandon is nonetheless a long drive of nearly fifty kilometres/thirty miles from Tralee, the largest town within the ambit of the peninsula. There is ample accommodation on or near the peninsula. Besides Tralee, Dingle is well placed but is a much smaller centre. The bus service to Dingle is frequent, but generally buses do not facilitate the best areas for walkers. The whole peninsula is mapped at a 1:50,000 scale by sheets 70 and 71.

Facilities and mapping in Iveragh: the N70 (Ring of Kerry Road) circumnavigates Iveragh and is of quite good quality. It also carries a useful local bus service which runs clockwise once a day in summer only, and which might be combined with other local bus services to facilitate A to B walks. The N71 from Killarney to Kenmare follows a highly scenic but tortuous route via Moll's Gap. Other minor roads cross high passes in remote country at Ballaghasheen and Ballaghbeama. All in all, the road network is little more than adequate and the bus network leaves a large gap in the centre of the peninsula.

Killarney is a large town and very crowded in summer. It is convenient to much of the best walks in Iveragh, though the remote end of the peninsula is a long eighty kilometres/fifty miles away. Other settlements on the N70 have plenty of accommodation but are much smaller than Killarney and little better placed for exploring the whole peninsula. There is a good network of youth hostels, some in remote, rugged areas, and hostel-to-hostel walks are just about possible.

Much of Iveragh, including the area east of Killarney, is well mapped at 1:50,000 by sheets 78 and 79. The bulk of the area covered by these two sheets is also mapped at a 1:25,000 scale (the area covered by the latter is not shown on the accompanying sketch map). The 1:25,000 maps are a doubtful investment since they give little more information than the 1:50,000 maps.

The western and southern parts of the peninsula have only half-inch maps (sheets 20 and 24) with an awkward border between them. In this regard, it is worth noting that the preliminary version of sheet 78 (1:50,000) extends five kilometres further west than the "Rambler" definitive version and so might be marginally more useful in this area.

Facilities and mapping in Beara: a moderately good road runs round Beara, and the spectacular Healy Pass Road crosses it about one-third from its eastern end. Kenmare, a comparatively large town, is a convenient centre both for the best of Beara and much of the south of Iveragh. Glengarriff and Adrigole are convenient to the south of the peninsula. There is a beautifully located youth hostel right in the heart of the mountains and another at the tip of the peninsula. No express bus serves the peninsula but there is a flexibly routed private bus service eastward along the southern side of the peninsula each morning, returning in the evening.

As well as the usual half-inch maps (most of the peninsula is on sheet 24, but 20 and 21 are also marginally useful), much of Beara is covered on an out-of-date one-inch map ("Kerry District"). A small area at its north-eastern corner is badly split between all three half-inch maps.

The entire peninsula is due to be mapped in the Discovery Series (1:50,000) in 1994.

Dingle

Route 106: East Dingle – Slieve Mish

Map 71 (1:50,000), preliminary edition.

Start at end of tarmac on side road off N86 (Q 741110). To get there, drive 5.1 miles west from Blennerville Bridge to hump-backed bridge and then take second road left (narrow!). Park considerately at turning point at end. Take initial path south, then leave it after 200 metres or so to cross river on left, climb Scragg, point 819 metres, Baurtregaum (trig pillar). Walk south-west to saddle and climb Caherconree. Walk north-west for 200 metres to avoid cliffs, then descend north to Gearhane (point 792 metres) and continue along its north-east spur to rejoin outward route.

Distance: 11 kilometres.   Climb: 950 metres.
Time: 4 hours.

Route 107: Central Dingle

Map 70 (1:50,000), preliminary edition (forested area shown south of Stradbally greatly exaggerated).

Start at Stradbally village (Q 592122). Take laneway to east of Courtney's pub and continue south along river valley to Lough Acummeen, climb Stradbally, Beenoskee (trig pillar), walk south-west for 500 metres, then north-west to climb Coumbaun, Beenatoor. Descend north spur, veering right off it to walk down river valley and reach road 2.5 kilometres west of start.

Distance: 13 kilometres.   Climb: 1,000 metres.
Time: 4.25 hours.

Route 108: West Dingle – Brandon

Map 70 (1:50,000), preliminary edition (area shown forested around Q 4711 greatly exaggerated).

To get there from Cloghane take minor road south-west for 2.2 miles to cross bridge over Owenmore River and start at next farm entrance on right (Q 490084). Walk path initially north-west, keeping on north-east side of pater-noster lakes and join main path near head of pater-noster corrie. Follow path to Brandon (trig pillar, ruins) turning left where steep ground eases. Walk south-east following wall and with cliffs on left, to Brandon Peak. Walk to Gearhane (narrow section of ridge rather than peak), descend generally south-east with cliff edge/steep ground on left to reach road at about Q 488077 (safeguard young trees on final descent). Walk road one kilometre to start.

Distance: 12 kilometres.   Climb: 1,100 metres.
Time: 4.25 hours.

Iveragh

Route 109: Iveragh – Purple Mountain Group

Rambler map 78 (1:50,000) or Killarney National Park map (1:25,000).

Start at car park at Kate Kearney's Cottage (V 881887). Walk north along road, cross bridge, take first road right. Ignore right turn after 300 metres to continue straight ahead on path which swings south on initial climb to Tomies Mountain. Keep to high ground to Purple Mountain (832 metres), retrace steps to point 757 metres and walk to Shehy north-east top (563 metres). Descend north-west for 500 metres to avoid cliffs, then north-east to reach forest track. Follow to road. Walk can be easily shortened, and final road walk eliminated, by returning onto initial path. Be extremely cautious if attempting a descent to the Gap of Dunloe as there are many sections of cliff.

Distance: 18 kilometres.   Climb: 1,000 metres.
Time: 5.5 hours.

Route 110: Reeks Ridge

Rambler map 78 (1:50,000) or MacGillycuddy's Reeks map (1:25,000).

Start at car park at end of road (V 836873), finish at car park at Kate Kearney's Cottage (V 881887) but note escape routes back to start over initially steep ground in following description. Walk track south, ascend steeply on path (Devil's Ladder) to col south-east of Carrauntoohil (careful – slippery when wet). Walk east, north-east with cliffs on left to Cnoc na Peiste (point 988 metres) – escape possible north-west. Some scrambling on north-east and north legs from here to Cruach Mhor (point 932 metres, grotto), worst avoided by veering right on first, left on second leg. (Escape possible north from Cruach Mhor on.) Walk east to point 731 metres, north-east to point 422 metres. At shallow col north meet path/track heading east to road.

Distance: 18 kilometres.   Climb: 1,250 metres.
Time: 6.75 hours (including 1 hour for steep ground and scrambling).

Route 111: Central Reeks

Rambler map 78 (1:50,000) or MacGillycuddy's Reeks map (1:25,000).

Start at bridge (V 767867) on minor road 1.6 miles south of prominent junction. Walk one hundred metres south-west along road, turn left to follow track/path with river on left. At about Lough Eighter climb north-west spur of Caher to its two summits (200 metres apart) and then follow cliffs on left to Carrauntoohil (trig pillar, cross). From summit, retrace steps south-west one hundred metres (most important to avoid cliffs!) and here descend steeply north-west to reach Beenkeragh ridge. Walk ridge to Beenkeragh (careful – some scrambling necessary on ridge especially at start, worst avoidable by keeping to left of crest). Climb Beenkeragh, Skregmore (three main summits), descend steeply close to Lough Eighter. Retrace steps to start.

Distance: 13 kilometres.   Climb: 1,250 metres.
Time: 5.75 hours (including 1 hour for scrambling and steep descent).

Route 112: North Iveragh

Rambler map 78 (1:50,000).

Start near right-angle bend to right on road at V 636852 (this road is signposted "Coomasaharn Lake" in Glenbeigh). Park considerately. Follow track south-west at this bend nearly to end, then climb steeply to Knocknaman. Walk south with cliffs on right, swinging west with cliffs to follow wall to

Coomacarrea. Climb Teermoyle Mountain (indistinct summit may be bypassed by following cliff on right), take narrow but safe arete eastwards over point 608 metres. Walk directly to road.

Distance: 10 kilometres.   Climb: 800 metres.
Time: 3.75 hours (including 0.25 hours for steep descent).

Route 113: Iveragh – Mullaghanattin

Rambler map 78 (1:50,000).

Start at junction on side road (V 718797). Walk south along track; at Cloghera ask permission to continue, climb to east side Eskabehy Lough and climb north spur of Mullaghanattin (trig pillar) to summit (some scrambling near top can be avoided by walking east from lake and ascending north spur of point 683 metres). Walk west to point 692 metres, bypassing small memorial on way and keep to high ground, going generally south-west, over point 752 metres (Beann) to point 543 metres. Descend to south side Coomloughra Lough (very slow going and difficult navigation), climb point 666 metres, point 532 metres. Descend to end of track at south-west corner of Cloon Lough. Track to start.

Distance: 18 kilometres.   Climb: 1,300 metres.
Time: 6.75 hours (including 1 hour for difficult terrain).

An easier and obvious circuit from the south, starting at the junction at V 747747, can be made traversing the peaks around the Pocket, including Mullaghanattin.

Distance: 10 kilometres.   Climb: 1,000 metres.
Time: 3.75 hours.

Route 114: West Iveragh

Rambler map 78 (1:50,000).

Start near concrete bridge (V 669712). Half-inch map and sheet 78 required to get there from Sneem but the following should suffice. Cross bridge westward in Sneem, fork right at green, take first road right, fork left at football field after 0.2 miles, turn left at T-junction after further 3.0 miles and drive 0.6 miles to concrete bridge. Park considerately. Walk track north from farm to end (this runs higher than shown on map), then cross stile just west of summit to reach Knocknagantee. Follow fence to near Knockmoyle, then continue to summit. Follow edge of steep ground south-east, initially following fence. Climb point 636 metres. Descend initially south, then south-west to rejoin initial track.

Distance: 10 kilometres.   Climb: 800 metres.
Time: 3.5 hours.

Route 115: Iveragh – Mangerton Group

Map 79 (1:50,000), preliminary edition.

Start at track's fork at end of side road (W 034839) – road

does not extend as far south as shown on map. Walk track south-east and cross gate at end. Head south-east into valley with cliffs on right (slow going), and climb south to Lough Nabroda. Walk to south end of Crohane Lough (forest shown on map on east side of lake does not exist), climb north to point 391 metres and continue to Bennaunmore (454 metres). Retrace steps to col between last two peaks climbed and descend steeply west through old oaks to valley (do not attempt descent west elsewhere). Walk north along right bank of river to above-mentioned gate and retrace steps.

Distance: 10 kilometres.   Climb: 500 metres.
Time: 4 hours (including 1 hour for difficult terrain).

Route 116: Iveragh – Mangerton

Rambler maps 78 and 79 (1:50,000), preliminary editions.

To get to start at W 005856 cross Owgarriff Bridge (W 007859) eastwards, take first right, drive 0.2 miles, park at bend left with bridge right. Walk across bridge, take centre gate immediately beyond and walk track/path to Lough Garagarry. Climb Stoompa from north-west spur, climb point 646 metres and continue, cliffs on right to Mangerton (trig pillar in flattish area of peat hags). Descend north-east (marker stones helpful) to spur east of Devil's Punch Bowl, climb point 782 metres and continue down to Lough Garagarry. Retrace steps to start.

Distance: 15 kilometres.   Climb: 900 metres.
Time: 4.5 hours.

Beara

Route 117: Shehy Mountains – Gougane Barra

Map 24 (half-inch), but map 85 (1:50,000), Discovery Series, when available.

Start near church on peninsula to right of road (W 091657). Walk west seventy metres on road, turning left at circular toilets onto track. Follow until it heads east, then leave it right for Foilstookeen (indefinite rocky top) and plateau to its west, where small lakes are useful for navigation. Continue round high ground, passing shallow gap (1,400 feet) on way to Bealick (useful cairn in area with few distinguishing summit features). Walk broad spur to its north-east, passing small lake in bogland (do not attempt descent right over cliffs on this leg). Descend steeply off end of spur to river, turn right here to pick up path on right bank. Follow it to houses, take road to start.

Distance: 11 kilometres. Climb: 550 metres.
Time: 3.5 hours (including 0.5 hours for
route-finding and difficult descent).

Route 118: North Beara

Kerry District map (one-inch), but map 84 (1:50,000), Discovery Series, when available.

Start on road close to bungalow on right (V 760559). To get there from junction of R571 with R754, drive 0.8 miles west on R571, turn left, turn right after 0.6 miles and drive for further 1.0 miles. Walk track beside bungalow; at convenient point climb Cummeennahillan, Knocknaveachal, Tooth Mountain (marks end of rocky terrain), Coomacloghane (trig pillar) and continue anti-clockwise on high ground, cliffs on left, to Curraghreague. Descend to col to north-east (not shown on map) and climb hill beyond to avoid bad vegetation on direct descent from col. Descend to ringfort and track.

Distance: 11 kilometres.   Climb: 750 metres.
Time: 4 hours (including 0.5 hours for
difficult going around cross-ways slabs).

Route 119: Central Beara

Kerry District map (one-inch), but maps 84 and 85 (1:50,000), Discovery Series, when available.

Start at end of tarmac close to Isaghbuderlick Waterfall (name is misleadingly located on map) 4.2 miles along minor road (V 851623). Cross stream about seventy metres down from waterfall. Climb to Cummeenanimma, keeping on left of spine to avoid worst of rough ground, south to Coomnadiha (trig pillar) (do not attempt direct descent to Cummeenadillure Lough), east and north-east to Knocknagorraveela.. Walk north-west to stream and follow it down.

Distance: 9 kilometres.   Climb: 750 metres.
Time: 4 hours (including 1 hour for difficult terrain).

Route 120: Central Beara – Hungry Hill

Kerry District map (one-inch), but map 84 (1:50,000),

Discovery Series, when available.

Start at Glanmore Youth Hostel (V 780545). Walk four kilometres south-west along road, turning left here onto side road. Take side road or river bank, then climb to point 1,519 feet, Glas Loughs, Hungry Hill (trig pillar). Descend north for 500 metres, then north-east (difficult rocky slabs) over Derryclancy, Coombane to top of Healy Pass. Walk road to north side of pass, then descend left (signposted) directly towards youth hostel, picking up track at later stage.

Distance: 15 kilometres.   Climb: 750 metres.
Time: 4.75 hours (including 0.5 hours for difficult going around cross-ways slabs).

Easier Routes in Dingle

Route 121

Map 71 (1:50,000) hardly necessary.

Slieve Mish Mountains: start as route 106, but follow the initial river as far as Derrymore Lough and return by same route. (Enclosed valley with attractive lakes.)

Route 122

Map 70 (1:50,000).

Brandon: start of route 108, but return at north-west end of pater-noster lakes or take path back to Faha (Q 4911) and thence directly to Cloghane.

Route 123

Map 70 (1:50,000).

Reach Mount Eagle by climbing along track from the north-east at Kildurrihy (Q 3500). Excellent views seaward to Blaskets and Skelligs.

Easier Routes in Iveragh

Route 124

Map 79 (1:50,000).

Walk Cappagh Glen (route 115) by taking in the valleys to the east or west of Bennaunmore (pottering area).

Route 125

Map 78 (1:50,000) or National Park map.

Kerry Way starting at Muckross House (V 970861), by Torc Waterfall to Galway's Bridge (splendid oak forest), returning on N71 and then via Dinish Island.

Route 126

Map 78 (1:50,000) hardly necessary.

The Lough Acoose area (V 7585) and the valley to its south using the Kerry Way and the road along the east side of the lake.

Route 127

No map needed.

Gap of Dunloe: start at Kate Kearney's Cottage (V 881887) and walk south into gap. Spectacular views of glacial spillway but rather crowded in summer.

Route 128

Map 78 (1:50,000).

Lough Adoolig area (about V 6274). Walk (mostly pathless) along south side of narrow, remote glacial valley as far as encircling cliffs on east. Height: about 250 metres.

Easier Routes in Beara

Route 129

Kerry District map (one-inch).

Cummeengeera: start at same point as route 118 but walk south-west to head of valley, returning by same route.

Route 130

Map 24 (half-inch).

Barley Lake area (about V 8856). Car park (and road to it) just north-east of lake not shown on map. Circle lake (mostly pathless) taking in Crossterry Mountain. Highest point: 350 metres.

Further Reading about Kerry

The Hills of Cork and Kerry, by Richard Mersey (Gill and Macmillan, 1987). Background and atmosphere rather than detailed guide.

South-West: New Irish Walks Guides by Sean O Suilleabhain (Gill and Macmillan, 1987). Forty-nine route descriptions.

West Cork Walks by Kevin Corcoran (O'Brien Press, 1991). Ten easy walks with emphasis on flora and fauna.

Kerry Walks by Kevin Corcoran (O'Brien Press, 1992). Twenty varied walks with emphasis on flora and fauna.

Walk Cork and Kerry by David Perrot and Joss Lynam (Batholomew, 1990). Forty mostly easy walks described in a very readable format.

Macgillycuddy's Reeks by John Murray (Dermot Boucher-Hayes Commemoration Trust, 1991). Twelve walks and a 1:25,000 map.

THE HIGHEST PEAKS

. . . .

In the following list of the thirty highest peaks in Ireland, note that the metric and imperial heights may not exactly correspond: the heights are taken without adjustment from metric and imperial maps. If only one height (metric or imperial) is recorded on the maps, the other is a calculated equivalent and this is noted in the following table by an asterisk.

What exactly constitutes a mountain and what only a high point on a ridge has been the subject of much lengthy dispute, which I have no intention of augmenting. Let it merely be said that there are several tops in the Reeks, and probably elsewhere, whose champions would certainly consider to be "true" mountains. Even without these doubtful tops, however, the dominance of the Kerry mountains in the following list is striking.

			HEIGHT	
RANK PEAK	REGION	(m)	(ft)
1 Carrauntoohil	Kerry (Iveragh)	1,039	3,414
2 Beenkeragh	Kerry (Iveragh)	1,010	3,314
3 Caher	Kerry (Iveragh)	1,001	3,200
4 Cnoc na Peiste	Kerry (Iveragh)	988	3,241*
5 Brandon	Kerry (Dingle)	952	3,127
6 Lugnaquillia	Wicklow	925	3,039
7 Galtymore	South-East (Galtees)	920*	3,018
8 Knockbrinnea	Kerry (Iveragh)	854	2,782
9 Baurtregaum	Kerry (Dingle)	851	2,796
9 Skregmore	Kerry (Iveragh)	851	2,790

11 Slieve Donard	N Ireland		
	(Mournes)	850	2,796
12 Mullaghcleevaun	Wicklow	847	2,788
13 Brandon Peak	Kerry (Dingle)	840	2,764
14 Mangerton	Kerry (Iveragh)	839	2,756
15 Caherconree	Kerry (Dingle)	835	2,713
16 Purple Mtn	Kerry (Iveragh)	832	2,739
17 Lyracappul	South-East (Galtees)	827*	2,712
18 Beenoskee	Kerry (Dingle)	826	2,713
19 Tonelagee	Wicklow	817	2,686
20 Mweelrea	Mayo	814	2,688
21 Nephin	Mayo	807*	2,646
22 Greenane	South-East (Galtees)	803*	2,636
22 Gearhane	Kerry (Dingle)	803	2,636
22 Ben Lugmore	Mayo (Mweelrea)	803	2,636
25 Galtybeg	South-East (Galtees)	801*	2,629
26 Clohernagh	Wicklow	800	2,623
27 Stradbally	Kerry (Dingle)	798	2,627
28 Mount Leinster	South-East		
	(Blackstairs)	796*	2,610
29 Knockmealdown	South-East		
	(Knockmealdowns)	795*	2,609
30 Fauscoum	South-East		
	(Comeraghs)	792*	2,597

BIBLIOGRAPHY

. . . .

While some of the following books are no longer in print, libraries should contain copies of all of them. There is a further list of books under each regional chapter.

Butterfield, Irvine, *The High Mountains of Britain and Ireland* (Diadem, 1988). Route descriptions of the Irish Munros.

Dillon, Paddy, *The Mountains of Ireland* (Cicerone, 1992). Guide to climbing all of Ireland's mountains over 2,000 feet.

Fewer, Michael, *Irish Long Distance Walks* (Gill and Macmillan, 1993). Detailed descriptions of all the waymarked long-distance walks.

Herman, David, *Great Walks Ireland* (Cassell, 1991). Thirty mountain walks in all areas of Ireland, with colour photographs.

Lynam, Joss (ed.), *Irish Peaks* (Constable, 1982). Fifty walks in every mountain area in Ireland, illustrated with black-and-white photographs.

Mulholland, H., *Guide to Ireland's 3,000-Foot Mountains* (Mulholland Wirral, 1988). Route descriptions for Irish Munros.

Pochin Mould, D.D.C., *The Mountains of Ireland,* 2nd edition (Gill and Macmillan, 1976). A general overview with black-and-white photographs, mostly aerial.

Wilson, Ken and Gilbert, Richard, *The Big Walks* (Diadem, 1980). Accounts of marathon walks in Wicklow, the Mournes, the Maamturks, the Reeks and Beara.

Wilson, Ken and Gilbert, Richard, *Classic Walks* (Diadem, 1982). Accounts of walks in Donegal, Sligo, Mweelrea, the Twelve Bens, the Galtees and Brandon.

Wilson, Ken and Gilbert, Richard, *Wild Walks* (Diadem, 1988). Accounts of walks in the Sperrins, west Iveragh, the Knockmealdowns, the Nephins, Slieve League and Mangerton.

USEFUL ADDRESSES

. . . .

An Oige – Youth Hostel Association of Ireland, 61 Mountjoy
Street, Dublin 1. (01) 304555.
Irish Budget Hostels, Doolin Village, Co. Clare. (065) 74006.
Independent Hostel Owners Ireland, Information Office,
Dooey Hostel, Glencolumcille, Co. Donegal. (073) 30130.
Youth Hostel Association of Northern Ireland, 56 Bradbury
Place, Belfast BT7 1RU. (0232) 324733.

Association for Adventure Sports, House of Sport, Longmile
Road, Dublin 12. (01) 509845.
Cospoir – National Sports Council, Hawkins House, Hawkins
Street, Dublin 2. (01) 8734700 (responsible for long-
distance walks).
Mountaineering Council of Ireland, House of Sport, Longmile
Road, Dublin 12. (01) 509845.
Sports Council for Northern Ireland, House of Sport, Upper
Malone Road, Belfast BT9 5LA. (0232) 381222.

Bord Failte Eireann – Irish Tourist Board, Baggot Street
Bridge, Dublin 2. (01) 6765871.
Northern Ireland Tourist Board, River House, 48 High Street,
Belfast BT1 2DS. (0232) 246609.

Ordnance Survey of Ireland, Phoenix Park, Dublin 8. (01) 8206100.

Ordnance Survey of Northern Ireland, Colby House, Stranmillis, Belfast BT9 5BJ. (0232) 661244.

Irish Rail, Head Office, Connolly Station, Dublin 1. (01) 366222.

Irish Bus – Bus Eireann, Broadstone, Dublin 7. (01) 366111.

Lough Swilly Bus Co., Head Office, Letterkenny, Co. Donegal. (074) 22400.

Northern Ireland Railways, Central Station, East Bridge Street, Belfast BT1. (0232) 230310.

Ulsterbus, Europa Bus Centre, Glengall Street, Belfast BT2. (0232) 333000.